Urban Walks

Urban Walks

23 Walks through Seattle's Parks and Neighborhoods

by Joan Burton and Duse McLean

Thistle Press

Urban Walks

Illustrations copyright © 2001
by Sheila Ralston

Downtown Walk Copyright © 2001
by Duse McLean

Cover illustration: Dave Albers

Book design: Magrit Baurecht

Maps: Desktop Connexion Inc

Library of Congress
Cataloging-in-Publication Data:
Urban walks : 23 walks through Seattle's parks and neighborhoods by Joan Burton co-author Duse McLean
      p.   cm.
Includes index
2001 130566

ISBN 0-9621935-9-3
      1. Seattle (Wash)—Tours. 2. Walking—Washington (State)—Seattle—Guidebooks.

Printed in the United States

For information about volume discounts, excerpts or illustrations contact:

THISTLE PRESS
P.O. Box 732
Bellevue, WA 98009
425-885-3173

CONTENTS

LAKE WASHINGTON

RENTON

QUICK REFERENCES

INDEX

ILLUSTRATIONS

Illustrations by Sheila Ralston

OTHER BOOKS FROM THISTLE PRESS

*The Pocket Guide to Seattle
and Surrounding Areas*

The Pioneers of Lake View

Seattle's Totem Poles

INTRODUCTION

Whether you are new to Seattle or a native, *Urban Walks* will introduce you to parts of the city you have never seen before. Our walks take you off your normal city routes — out of gridlocked traffic and crowded arterials — allowing you to see the living city.

Visitors and residents can never see enough of Seattle's natural beauty — and it is all the more apparent when you are on foot. Short walks are the key. Few of these walks take more than three hours; most are less than that.

Unlike surrounding suburbs, many Seattle neighborhoods started as separate towns in early days and have evolved into unique and distinct communities. Why not take a look at them on foot? Our city history is short; our oldest buildings go back only a century. By walking you can see architectural details and landscaping in ways not possible from a car. It is easy to imagine the lives of Seattle's first settlers in their new land if you visit our old-growth parks and walk our city shorelines. How fortunate we are that so much has been preserved and is accessible.

So — put on your walking shoes and start by simply putting one foot in front of the other. Happy walking!

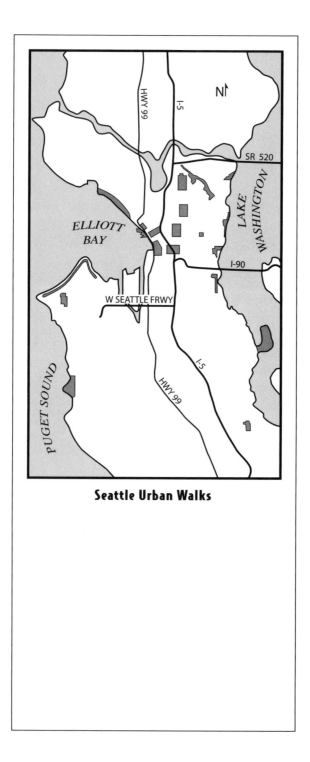

Seattle Urban Walks

GETTING STARTED

A city is an dynamic entity. Buildings are replaced, earthquakes strike, plans fall through. Inevitably things will change after this book's publication. We have tried to show a cross section of Seattle, walks that locals as well as visitors might do to see, understand and enjoy our city and its history.

Each walk has basic information about the walk, the history of the area and guided directions for the route. The top section of each chapter gives the hard facts about the walk, as does the chart on pages 200–201. It's a good idea to carry a small backpack with water and perhaps a snack, as well as an extra sweater or light jacket for Seattle's unpredictable weather, and any other necessities. Comfortable shoes are a requirement in any weather.

If you plan to take a Metro bus, please call Metro (206-553-3000) to confirm their schedule and stops. Routes and schedules are subject to change. Parking is available near most parks, but in some seasons it may be difficult – i.e., it is impossible to get anywhere near Alki on a sunny Sunday in the summer. And, remember, you're going on a walk – take your time.

Many of these walks may be joined together to make longer walks, or rearranged, if you would like to devise your own route. That's the pleasure of walking. Times for walks are estimates, to give you an idea of how long the walking part of the walk might be relative to other walks. We haven't factored in sitting on

a beach to enjoy the view or stopping for a latte or bite to eat. Most walks are wheel chair or stroller accessible, although a few of the hilly trails are not. The best are the broad, level walks, as noted in the chart on pages 200–201. Also, dogs on leash could accompany a walker on most walks, but information on the best trails for pets is included in the walks and on the chart. Please be considerate and take a pooper scooper along (it's the law).

Always use common sense. Parks and neighborhoods that are fine during the day may not be safe in evenings or after dark. If something doesn't feel right, save it for another day.

As we wrote this book, we realized we had only begun to explore the possibilities of walks in Seattle. We selected these walks as representative of parks and neighborhoods but know you, the reader, may have favorites we have missed. Please let us know your ideas.

SEATTLE'S OLMSTED PARKS

"I do not know of any place where the natural advantages for parks are better than here. They can be made very attractive and will be, in time, one of the things that will make Seattle known all over the world."

– Quote from John Charles Olmsted upon his first visit to Seattle. From an article in the Seattle *Post-Intelligencer,* May 1, 1903

Seattle is blessed by its beautiful location, but it was its visionary citizens who recognized that parks celebrating the landscape would enhance it.

Being a young city, Seattle could learn from older cities in the Northeast about what made them attractive and livable – and parks in Boston and New York designed by the Olmsted firm were notable examples. At the beginning of the twentieth century large tracts of recently logged land were just being developed, plans were forming to lower Lake Washington, and civic pride and prosperity was at its height from the Klondike Gold Rush. Riding on the "City Beautiful" movement that was sweeping the country, Seattle's boosters took up the cause for a major park and boulevard system designed by the eminent Olmsted Brothers firm. Frederick Law Olmsted, known as the father of landscape architecture, had designed Central Park in New York City in the mid–1800s and was a strong advocate of parks as a civilizing and healthy influence for cities. Olmsted's son, Frederick Law Olmsted, Jr., and stepson-nephew, John Charles Olmsted, joined the firm in the late 1800s and carried on its work, with John Charles doing most of the planning in Seattle.

John Charles Olmsted had been invited to Seattle by the Board of Park Commissioners in the spring of 1903 to prepare a report on how to beautify the city with a comprehensive system of parks and boulevards. The Seattle *Post-Intelligencer* covered his visit extensively and enthusiastically, helping to gain public support for the many projects, which included playgrounds and a year round recreation system as well as parks and boulevards. He submitted his report in October of that year. The City Council adopted his report and created an independent Parks Department to begin implementing the plan soon after. Work started with the parks the city already owned and continued on parks added to the system through the years.

His enthusiasm for the area shows in an early statement from the newspaper: "I do not know of any place where the natural advantages for parks are better than here. They can be made very attractive and will be, in time, one of the things that will make Seattle known all over the world." [Seattle *Post-Intelligencer,* May 1, 1903] John Charles not only appreciated the city's great natural setting, but also the differences in terrain, neighborhoods and purpose of the various parks. He advocated creating parks that fit in unobtrusively to their surroundings, while preserving as much as possible "the advantages of water and mountain views and of woodlands, well distributed and conveniently located." [Olmsted Report]

The key to the plan, John Charles believed, was the boulevard system throughout the city that would provide pleasant drives and link together its many parks. Parks and playgrounds would not only enhance the city, but also property values, by creating an ambiance and opportunities for healthful living.

In addition to private gardens and entire neighborhoods, Seattle has thirty-five Olmsted parks, the University of Washington campus, and the Washington Park Arboretum, linked together by an extensive boulevard system ringing the city, leaving some of the area's most stunning vistas and landscapes open for all to see. Maintaining and enhancing the Olmsted vision is a process that continues to this day. As you walk through the urban paths of Seattle, give a thought to how they might have looked without the invaluable Olmsted influence.

For more information see the Olmsted Exhibit at the top of the Water Tower in Volunteer Park or contact the Seattle Parks Department (206-684-4075) or the Friends of Olmsted Parks (P.O. Box 9884, Seattle, WA 98109) for a brochure and information.

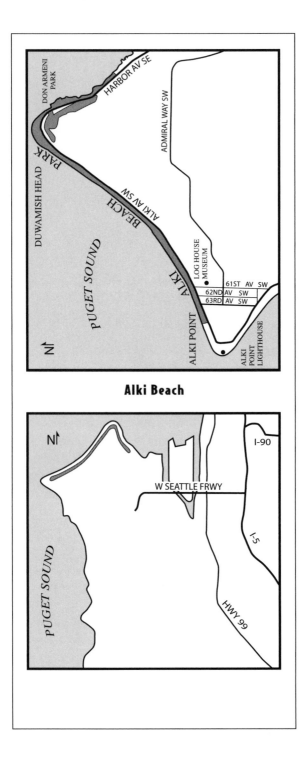

Alki Beach

ALKI BEACH

Distance	6+ miles round trip
Time	2-3 hours
Terrain	A broad level walkway
Restrooms	2 along the beach
Food	Restaurants nearby

*Y*achts and ferries fill the waters where Seattle's pioneers traveled to their new home in 1851. Once the home of local Duwamish and Suquamish Indians, this popular beach pulses with activity in the summer and offers spectacular views anytime.

Getting There

By Car: From the north, take I-5 to the West Seattle freeway, exit #163A. Drive west to Harbor Avenue. (Or turn right off Southwest Spokane Street onto Harbor Avenue Southwest.) Follow Harbor Avenue to the beginning of the paved walkway at California Avenue Southwest. Park along the road just beyond Salty's restaurant.

Metro: Bus #37 stops at Southwest California Way and Harbor Avenue.

Background

Seattle's first settlers finally arrived on a cold, windy wet November day in 1851. Lured west by the promise of fertile lands, a mild climate and donation claims, the group had set out from their homes in Illinois by wagon train the preceding spring. They stopped briefly in Portland before establishing their settlement in the present-day West Seattle. The twenty-four first settlers, Dennys, Borens, Bells, Lows and the Terry brothers, settled in quickly, building cabins for their families and learning to eat the new diet the local Indians showed them: clam juice, salmon, wild game and native berries. New Yorker Charles Terry envisioned a great future for their humble settlement and named it New York-Alki. ("Alki" meant "bye-and-bye" in the Salish language and was pronounced "al-kee." During prohibition the pronunciation was changed to "alk-eye" to avoid confusion with the nickname for an alcoholic drink.) The following spring the families moved across Elliott Bay to a more sheltered harbor out of the cold wind, where they established their claims and began logging the land. Only Charles Terry and the John Low family stayed over on Alki and made their claims there. A few years later Terry changed his mind and traded claims with Doc Maynard for his claim in present-day Pioneer Square and the Lows moved to the Olympia area to farm.

Unlike most of Seattle's early parks, Alki Beach was not originally accessible by street car, but only by water. By 1889 the ferry from Seattle brought as many as 2,000 people to Alki on weekends for daytime beach outings. At the turn of the century only a few summer camps had been built along the shore. By 1902 West Seattle had incorporated as a city and Alki had become so popular that a trolley line was extended to the area, finally making land access possible. Its finest moment may have been in 1902 when L. G. Mecklem rose into the sky from the shores of Alki in a heated air balloon and blew across the Duwamish River to Georgetown. Two years later the city purchased the beach strip between Fifty-eighth and Sixty-fifth streets, creating the first municipal saltwater beach on the West Coast.

After a series of city condemnations and acquisitions, Alki Beach Park became the city's first waterfront beach park in 1911. The park's original design was influenced by the Olmsteds, who designed so many of Seattle's parks.

By then, Alki had become a resort, with a first class hotel and a grand Coney Island-style amusement park called Luna Park. Opened in 1907, this was an enormously popular outdoor amusement area, where throngs came to ride the roller coaster, go to the theater or movie house, dance, and "bathe" in an indoor saltwater natatorium. Known as "the greatest amusement park in the Northwest," it was also infamous for its well-stocked bar, which attracted a rowdy clientele. Under the shadow of civic scandals and changing times, the park gradually faded after 1913 and was torn down. The remnants of the resort burned down in 1931, and in 1945 the area became a small public park, now almost forgotten. Today when the tide is low you can see the stubs of pilings remaining from turn-of-the-century amusement centers.

West Seattle annexed to Seattle in 1907, with most of its business catering to the tourists coming to its beaches. By 1909 transient campers had built log cabins, cottages and tents in local West Seattle farms. A writer at the time said that "for three solid miles shacks and camps and cottages are so near together that it amounts to practically a solid block."

After the Depression and War years Seattle's suburbs grew mainly to the east, as the Lake Washington bridges provided accessibility. West Seattle was almost forgotten, especially as its bridges became clogged. Traffic was further impeded when an off-course tug struck a pylon in 1978, leaving half the bridge stuck in the open position for years. But Alki has been rediscovered recently with posh new condominiums and apartment buildings replacing modest beach cottages from the 1920s and 1930s. Look behind the buildings at the steep hills that collapsed during recent landslides; you can see the city's efforts to stabilize the hillsides with new walls and plantings.

The Walk

Note: This is a long walk and can be easily broken into segments.

Start just beyond Salty's restaurant. In many places you will have a choice between the broad sidewalk along the road or smaller paths along the beach. We recommend the beach path for its views and much quieter atmosphere. Look for historic plaques imbedded in sidewalks, walls and monuments along the way. Dogs may be walked on leash along the paths but are prohibited from the beach.

The magnificent crescent-shaped waterfront feels a bit like a transplanted California beach. The entire paved walk is close to water level, with only beach grass, shrubs, and wild roses huddled beneath occasional windswept trees along the promenade. Stairways in the seawall lead to the beach below. When the tide is in and waves are pounding, the stairs seem incongruous, but in any weather the views are glorious. Swimmers brave the cold Puget Sound waters here throughout the year. A city project to enhance the shoreline has added viewing platforms and telescopes along the way, some with superimposed historic scenes on top of current views. Scuba divers use these sheltered coves to launch their explorations – you may see their flags floating near the shore.

As you walk along the first coves stop and listen for a moment: You'll hear sea lions barking in the water, cormorants and gulls calling out, and waves lapping at the shore, juxtaposed with the noises of our urban environment just feet away. Look for such marine birds as loons, goldeneyes, grebes, cormorants, and buffleheads, along with the ever-present mallards and gulls.

Walk northwest along the shore past fishing piers and a boat rental shop to Don Armeni Park, named for a sheriff's deputy who died in the line of duty. Grateful West Seattleites erected the monument and set aside this park in his memory.

Round the point and you are at Duwamish Head. Your view is northeast to the Space Needle, downtown skyscrapers, and mountains beyond. By twilight as city lights come on the effect is magical. Before the white setters arrived, this area was the site of a Duwamish fishing camp know as Squdux. In September of 1851 David Denny, John Low and Lee Terry were dropped off here to explore the area for their future home and were welcomed by an encampment of Indians. Low laid claim to the beach west of Squdux and returned to Portland to get his family. David Denny sent along a note to his brother Arthur to bring the rest of the group to the area, saying, "We have examined the valley of the Duwamish River and find it a fine country. There is plenty of room for one thousand settlers. Come at once."

As you continue, Harbor Avenue becomes Alki Avenue. Plaques in the pavement identify this tiny point of land as the location of the grand amusement park, Luna Park. Look for a huge rusty anchor recovered from an unidentified ship in the bay.

Continue around the point; you are walking west, turning your back on the hills of Magnolia and Queen Anne and facing the islands in the sound and the Olympic Mountains beyond. At Alki Avenue Southwest the shoreline expands to a wide sandy beach, Alki Beach Park, with driftwood and large concrete fire pits, used year round for beach picnics. In summer nets are strung for impromptu volley ball games. Look for an old bathhouse converted to an art studio run by the Alki Community Center.

Continue on the promenade to a miniature version of the Statue of Liberty at the foot of Sixty-first Avenue, a gift from a local Boy Scout troop. Various interpretive signs, artistic and historic interpretive tiles, and memorials along the promenade explain Indian names, Indian culture, the geologic effect of the Vashon Glacier on Puget Sound, and more recently, the landing of the schooner Exact in 1851 at the "birthplace of Seattle."

Across the street several ethnic and American restaurants, coffee shops, and bakeries have unobstructed views of the Sound. Take a short detour from the beach at Sixty-first Avenue to the venerable Alki Homestead Restaurant, which has served family dinners since 1950. The traditional old log house was the main house. One block farther east, at the corner of Sixty-first Avenue Southwest and Southwest Stevens, the Log House Museum was John G. Maurer's carriage house, built in 1903 with timbers rescued from Puget Sound after he came back from the Alaska Gold Rush. Historic photos and articles of Alki's history

line its walls. Operated by the Southwest Seattle Historical Society, it is open Thursday-Sunday; call 206- 938-5293 to check on hours.

Return to the beach and continue heading west. An obelisk monument at Sixty-third Avenue Southwest engraved with the names of Seattle's first twenty-four settlers commemorates their arrival on November 18, 1851. The scenic walkway ends abruptly at Alki Point but continue walking another two blocks past the homes and condos to the historic Alki Point Lighthouse, dating from 1912. (The narrow sidewalk disappears under parked cars, so you may want to cross the street.) At the turn of the century its oil lamp warned Mosquito Fleet steamships traveling between Seattle and Tacoma at night. In 1939 the U.S. Coast Guard took over lighthouse's operation, replacing the original lantern hung over a pole with the present light. It is open to tours from 12:00 to 3:30 on weekends only, but its colorful red roof and historic shape are worth a close-up look whenever you arrive.

Continue around the turn onto Beach Drive, where another walkway begins. You'll see freighters transporting goods, sailboats enjoying the breezes, and an expansive view of Puget Sound. And, if you're lucky, you may even catch a glimpse of Mount Rainier behind the ridge.

Look for brass constellation inlays along the sidewalk which signal the beginning of Constellation Park along the beach front. Follow the sidewalk down to the beach where the tiles of the seawall have drawings and identifications of sea and plant life found in the inter-tidal zones. Continue on around the bend to Cormorant, another beachfront park.

Return to your car or bus along the same route, seeing views and historic markers from the other direction.

NOTES

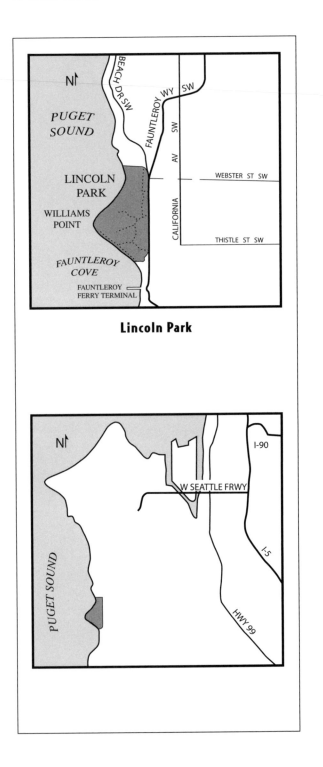

Lincoln Park

LINCOLN PARK

Distance	1¾ miles
Time	2 hours
Terrain	Varied – wide paved paths and narrow steep trails
Restrooms	At street level and on the beach
Food	No

One of Seattle's largest parks, Lincoln Park is also one of its most varied. Wooded paths lead through mature trees and pass by playfields and picnic tables, finally ending at a pebbly Puget Sound beach far below.

Getting There

By Car: From I-5 take exit #163A to the West Seattle freeway, staying left for West Seattle. Follow the signs to Fauntleroy Avenue South-west and the ferry. At the end of the freeway, stay on Fauntleroy as it curves to the left. The road bears left and crosses Alaska Street, and California Avenue. Go about two miles. The park is on the right at Southwest Webster. Park in the first parking lot (the north lot).

Metro: Take bus #54 to Southwest Fauntleroy and Southwest Webster.

Background

Lincoln Park, located about two miles south of Alki Point, took a long time to become a reality. When the Olmsteds first proposed a park here in 1903, West Seattle was outside the city limits so no action was taken. In 1912, after West Seattle had been absorbed into Seattle, local boosters promoted a woodland and beach park at this location and invited the Seattle Park Board to a picnic at Williams Point. The promotion was effective, but it took until 1922 for the City Council to finally appropriate money to purchase the 120 acres that make up Lincoln Park. The saltwater pool was built on the site of a lagoon on Williams Point. Heirs of Lawrence Colman, a Fauntleroy pioneer, gave Colman Pool to the city as a memorial to him.

Fauntleroy Cove was named in 1857 by Lieutenant Davidson for his future father in-law. This park was also supposed to be named for him. However, the City Park Board had planned to honor President Lincoln by naming one of the city's major parks for him and chose this one, so it received his name instead.

After purchasing the park land the Parks Department began removing houses and shacks scattered along the beach, and brush and downed timber were cleared from the woodland. Much of the initial clearing of the land was done during the Depression by men hired by the federal Works Progress Administration and State Civilian Conservation Corps.

The Walk

Lincoln Park lies on a high bluff in West Seattle overlooking Puget Sound. Below, the cobbled shore is a salt water beach extending a mile along the Sound. Inside the breakwater the spacious beach has picnic tables, barbeque pits and Colman Pool, an unusual outdoor salt-water swimming pool. In summer as you walk the wooded paths above, the sounds of swimmers and children playing far below float up the bluff. Nearly five miles of paths or trails wander through the woods, down the hill, and include a paved beach walk that ends near the Fauntleroy ferry landing to the south. Bird-lovers enjoy this park because of the variety of birds it attracts. Look for eagles in the tall trees waiting for their salmon dinner to swim by in the waters below.

Begin at the north parking lot on Fauntleroy Way opposite Southwest Webster Street, and head straight west toward the windswept trail along the bluff overlooking the Sound. You will come to the intersection of the broad bluff trail, with a choice of north or south vantages. It makes no difference which direction you choose, since you can descend to the water in either direction, but the steepest descent is in the center. Along the edge of the bluff are benches where you may rest and enjoy views of the Olympic Mountains, boats and ships, and the islands in the Sound through the red-barked madrona trees on the slope. Crows along the paths and gulls below compete loudly for attention.

Eventually you will want to drop down to the beach level and Colman Pool, the bath-house and the curious underground restrooms. The pool is open only during summer months; a small fee is charged. Picnic tables can be found throughout the park, and those close to

the pool are particularly popular. Since no food is available to buy, bring a snack or your own picnic.

Follow the wide paved path along Stony Beach at water level. On a windy day the surf swirls and foams beside you, and on a warm calm one, children play in the waves. From the south end of the park you can see the Fauntleroy ferry dock just around the corner.

Note: There are many paths, ranging from wide, paved stroller- and wheelchair-accessible to narrow trails. Unfortunately, there are no park maps. You may make this a short stroll on level ground or a more extended and energetic walk through the trails down to the water. A canine companion on leash would enjoy this walk.

Return to your car or bus along a different path.

NOTES

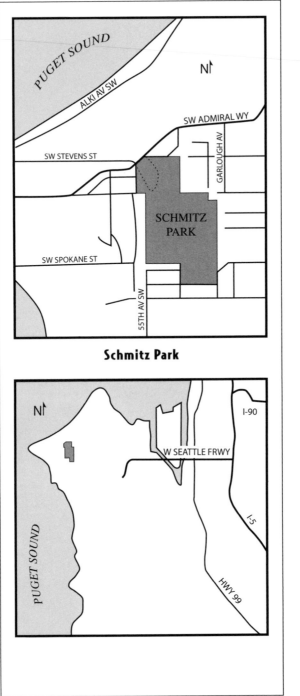

Schmitz Park

SCHMITZ PARK

Distance	1–2 miles
Time	1 hour
Terrain	Hilly trails
Restrooms	No
Food	No

This small forest park is tucked in the midst of a residential neighborhood. Sun filters through the limbs of the tall trees far above, while a stream meanders around stumps and logs below.

Getting There

By Car: Take I-5, to Exit #163A for West Seattle. Follow the signs for Southwest Admiral Way. Stay on Admiral and go over the top of the hill and down. Just after the second curve, at the intersection of South Stevens Street, turn left into the park entrance. The entrance road winds down a ravine to the parking area.

   Note: The entrance to the park is easy to miss. As you drive down Admiral Way begin to slow down after crossing Garlough Avenue and then move to the center, turning lane. The entrance to Schmitz is on the left, marked by a small Parks Department sign.

Metro: Take bus #56 and get off at the Schmitz Park entrance on Southwest Admiral Way. Drop down into the bowl-shaped, green, cathedral-like park.

Background

Like all the Northwest, this area was logged by the early settlers, but the biggest trees now standing may have been spared because they were too small at the time. Ferdinand and Emma Schmitz donated the first twenty-three acres for this park in 1908 to be used as a natural preserve, a relic of the old-growth forests they had homesteaded in the 1880s. Later, family members added to the park holdings and the city and school districts have taken some area away so that it now comprises 50 woodland acres.

Little remains of the original Olmsted design, which had a pergola and comfort station, with paths from the park connecting to Alki beach. Like other area parks, West Seattle's parks were originally the work of developers seeking to attract buyers to their new tracts. It worked. The park and beach were extremely popular in the early 1900s, drawing people from Seattle, first by ferry and later by trolley, to bathe, attend concerts, and go on rides in the nearby amusement park.

Vandalism and overuse have taken their toll, with damage to plants, trails, and the pergola, which was removed in 1948. Since then park policy has been to maintain the park as a "Natural Preserve" as mandated by the deed from the Schmitz family "...to be used perpetually...for park purposes...in order that certain natural features be preserved."

The Walk

A short drive from today's urban downtown leads to a reminder of the rugged terrain the pioneers settled. This walk is more like a mountain trail, with some rough terrain, so wear appropriate shoes.

Near the trailhead you can find a 1976 marker among the young Douglas fir trees planted by children of nearby Schmitz School to commemorate the country's 200th anniversary. There are two main loop trails that wind along the ravine and several smaller trails that lead deep into the woods. Walk alongside woodland vistas in every direction. Most of the large trees are second growth, and even those are enormous. Huge firs, Western red cedars, hemlocks, and alders tower over the trails, or have fallen nearby. Many are wrapped in moss, which provides nourishment for the small ferns growing overhead on the tree trunks. The effect of these ferns hanging from limbs far above is semi-tropical, almost like a mini-rain forest. Small trees grow from downed logs called nurse logs. Other trees are filled with cavities made by hungry woodpeckers digging for bugs. If you listen, you may hear one at work.

Be prepared to climb over fallen logs and wind around their velvet green stumps. Small streams and rapids gurgle alongside many of the trails, especially in rainy months. The paths eventually end at the rim of the ravine where homes begin. When Woodland Park Zoo horticulture experts were planning the Trail of Vines exhibit, they made a field trip to Schmitz Park to observe temperate forest vines. They even borrowed a few to incorporate into the new exhibit!

From the parking lot you can walk toward the Sound along the original road, now closed

to cars. The massive trees end abruptly on the other side of the overhead bridge, and the Schmitz Park magic seems to evaporate.

As you return to your car give thanks to Emma and Ferdinand Schmitz who immigrated from Germany in the 1880s and gave their land so that visitors can still experience the wilderness and giant trees that greeted Seattle's first settlers.

NOTES

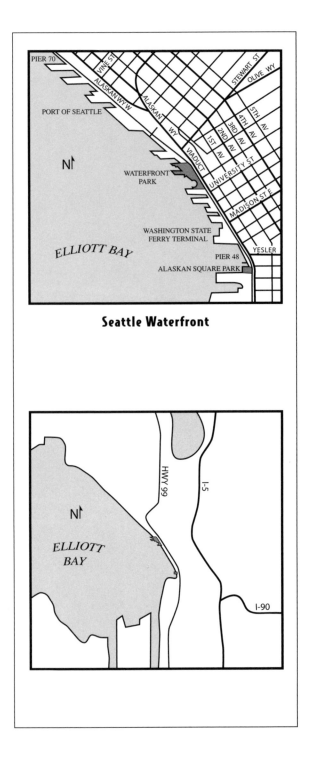

Seattle Waterfront

THE
WATERFRONT

Distance	1¼ miles one way
Time	1 hour
Terrain	Level
Restrooms	Most piers
Food	Pier restaurants along the way

Hard-working dock workers used to load ships docked along Seattle's waterfront, sending Northwest timber, coal and fish to far-flung ports. Now the piers are filled with tourist attractions, and cruise ships and ferries transport travelers to distant vacations and nearby towns.

Getting There

By Car: Drive to Alaskan Way at Pier 48 (Main Street) and park under the Alaskan Way Viaduct.

The Waterfront Streetcar runs the length of the Waterfront from Broad Street on the north to the International District (Jackson and Fifth Avenue) on the south with several stops along the way. A ticket is good for two hours, allowing time to get off and on. A bus transfer will be accepted on the streetcar, and vice versa.

Background

Like most nineteenth century port cities, Seattle's life revolved around its waterfront. Home of its first business, Henry Yesler's sawmill, the waterfront was the city's commercial hub for more than 100 years. Transcontinental railroad companies laid their tracks where the viaduct now stands so they could move their cargoes directly onto ships. There was so much commerce the street was named Railroad Avenue. Later, the name was changed to Alaskan Way because of the importance of trade with Alaska during and after the Klondike Gold Rush when the "Mosquito Fleet" carried goods and passengers throughout the Northwest. These little steamers and barges carried mail and, for decades, were a vital communication and transportation link for local river communities and Puget Sound destinations.

Pioneers Denny, Boren and Bell spent their first winter in the Northwest at "New York Alki" (present-day West Seattle), then explored Elliott Bay in the spring of 1852 in search of a more sheltered harbor. Challenged by the bay's steep cliffs to the north, they settled on the mud flats at the south end, and soon persuaded Henry Yesler to locate his steam sawmill here. It provided a vital source of income for the little village, while its chips and sawdust filled in the lagoon alongside the mill. Ships from San Francisco dumped their ballast into the bay, extending the waterfront and creating Ballast Island where the Kingdome recently stood. Today's waterfront is all on filled-in earth – behind a man-made breakwater. The original waterfront was the cliffs and hills above.

Northwest towns counted on railroads to link them to the outside world. When the

Northern Pacific selected Tacoma over Seattle, indignant Seattle citizens built their own railroad, the Seattle & Walla Walla, along the waterfront. Though it didn't get far, it did transport coal from Renton to waiting cargo ships in Elliott Bay.

Eventually, the railroad did come to Seattle, with James J. Hill's Great Northern in the 1880s. Soon owners of waterfront businesses built tracks to their piers along Railroad Avenue. At the turn of the century the Moran Boat Works built the agile little boats known as the Mosquito Fleet from their docks at the south end. Other docks were used for shipping, fishing fleets and canneries.

When ships began using containers for goods, commercial facilities moved south to the Harbor Island area, where ever bigger container cranes loom over the water. Gradually, the waterfront has been transformed into a tourist mecca, home to ferries, tour boats, cruise ships and various attractions.

The Walk

Be prepared for wind, even on a sunny day, the pungent smells of salt and creosote, and the demanding cries of gulls as they beg for snacks. Historic plaques along the sea wall point out places of significance as you walk. There are restaurants and snack bars all along the way. Waterfront merchants loan bright blue umbrellas to protect visitors from the elements on wet days; pick up one at the beginning of your walk and turn it in at another stop when you're done.

Begin at Pier 48, the site of the 1886 mass deportation of Seattle's Chinese immigrants. Subsequent coal docks and shipyards have been replaced by container ship docks south of the pier. The Port of Seattle has three periscopes on the end of Pier 48 that provide a terrific view of the Port's container terminals when the pier is open. One of the largest container ports in the nation, Seattle's working harbor is always busy.

Head north to the small park next door – known as Alaska Square – on the north side of the pier. A plaque at the base of the Tlingit totem pole describes Seattle's long ties to Alaska. The Washington Street Boat Landing where the Indians brought their canoes to sell crafts and salmon to settlers sits above a small public dock. The present pergola at the foot of Washington Street, built in 1920, has a plaque that tells about the side-wheel steamer *Idaho,* a wayside mission hospital ship that sank here and was buried when the harbor was filled in.

Walk north to Yesler Way, named for Henry Yesler, whose sawmill and dock were on this street. After the logs were milled they were sent to his wharf next door to be shipped out. The 900-foot wharf was later replaced by the Alaska Steamship Company wharf, also now gone. Yesler's first sawmill, built in 1852, brought vital business to the pioneer settlers.

Colman Dock, the present Washington State Ferry Terminal, Piers 50 and 52, was named for James Colman, the coal tycoon who brought Renton's coal out to the waterfront on the narrow-gauge Seattle & Walla Walla Railroad. Twice before the fire in 1889 and four times after, the dock has been rebuilt. In 1912 an ocean liner, the *Alameda,* knocked Colman Dock's clock tower into the bay. From 1892 through the 1920s a small steamer, the *Flyer,* took commuters and tourists around the Sound from Colman Dock. Starting in 1935, the private Black Ball Ferry Line ran a fleet of ferries imported from California around the Sound, which continued until

1951. At that point the State of Washington took them over, along with Colman Dock. The Black Ball line offered six daily trips and passenger, cargo, and mail service to communities on the Kitsap Peninsula, such as Suquamish and Indianola. The pride of the Black Ball Line was the *Kalakala,* a steel-hulled streamlined ferry, recently returned to this area for renovation after 30 years in Alaska.

When the state took over the ferries, many riders expected that cross-Sound bridges would soon make ferries obsolete. With the exception of the Agate Pass and Hood Canal bridges, this has not occurred. Super-ferries now provide frequent service to Bainbridge Island and Bremerton. The passenger-only ferries to Bremerton and Vashon Island leave from Pier 50 on the south side of Colman Dock. Like Yesler's Wharf, Pier 52 was also once 900 feet long and very grand, but is now 705 feet and handles Bainbridge Island and Bremerton car traffic. Water gurgles over a bronze sculpture by George Tsutakawa in front of the building.

The Ferry Terminal and holding dock occupy space that was the home of the Grand Trunk Pacific pier, which burned in 1914 in the second most dramatic fire in city history. Next to it was a terminal for the Mosquito Fleet. Both piers were razed in 1964 for the present Ferry Terminal.

Continue walking north, past the car holding area, to Pier 54, which contains Fire Station #5. Seattle's colorful fireboats are tied up at its docks, tucked away behind the building. The fireboat *Duwamish* built in 1909 was housed here, replaced in 1984 by the fireboats *Chief Seattle* and the *Alki*. The station's vintage fire engines are on display most afternoons.

Pier 54 is also the site of Ye Olde Curiosity Shop, opened in 1899, which feels like a quaint museum. Generations of children have inspected its mummy, shrunken human heads, duck-billed platypus, and the Lord's Prayer engraved on a pin.

Ivar Haglund opened his original restaurant and aquarium here in 1938. A statue of him feeding larger-than-life seagulls sits outside Ivar's Acres of Clams restaurant, a Seattle institution. The colorful Ivar, whose motto was "Keep Clam!" sang,

"I've traveled all over this country
And I say that if man ever found,
A place that is peaceful and quiet,
That spot is on Puget Sound."

The trolley stop is named "Clam Central Station" in his honor.

Pier 54 was the original Northern Pacific Pier 3 which extended along the waterfront between Madison and University streets. Its first tenants were James Galbraith & Cecil Bacon, who used this wharf for ships of the Mosquito Fleet. Later it was the Elliott Bay port of the Kitsap Transportation Company, which had steamers *Hyak, Kitsap, Reliance,* and *Utopia* working around Puget Sound. After World War II the piers were renumbered as 54-56.

You may wish to take a brief walk off the waterfront beneath the viaduct on Madison Street to Waterfront Place, a medley of old and new buildings, some with shops catering to tourists, and a variety of cafes.

Back on the waterfront continue walking north to Pier 55, which has tourist shops and sightseeing boats, including the Tillicum Village tours. Elliott's Restaurant on the north side of the pier is another popular waterfront restaurant.

Pier 55 and 56 housed ocean steamers providing passage to Antwerp, Havre, London, Cork, Mexico, San Francisco and the Mediterranean. The Alaska Commercial Company's steamers *Portland, St. Paul,* and the *Bertha* carried people north to Nome. Pier 56 was originally known as the Arlington Dock, and it was on this pier that President Teddy Roosevelt arrived in Seattle in 1903 for an enormous popular reception.

Next door, Pier 57, known as the Bay Pavilion, has shops, restaurants, public restrooms, a carousel and jazz concerts on Saturday afternoons. To its north is Waterfront Park, a public open space and maritime park where children can throw food to seagulls or fish in Elliott Bay. From waterside benches in the park you can watch the ferries, container ships and tugboats with barges. The 1889 fire damaged or destroyed homes and parts of hotels and a church here on the waterfront. This wharf was once known as Schwabacher's Wharf. On July 17, 1897, the SS *Portland* arrived here from the Klondike bearing the legendary "ton of gold," galvanizing Seattle's population and changing the waterfront forever.

You may wish to take a brief detour to the east from Pier 57. A short one-block walk on University Street goes to Western Avenue at the bottom of the elegant waterfall-lined Harbor Steps, designed by Arthur Erickson. The Seattle Art Museum is at the top of the stairs at First Avenue and the new Benaroya Hall, one block farther, at Second Avenue.

Back on the waterfront, continue walking north past Waterfront Park and the controversial statue of Christopher Columbus to Pier 59, home of the IMAXDome and the Seattle Aquarium. The IMAXDome features a large curved screen showing nature films, such as "The Eruption of Mount St. Helens" and "The Living Sea." The Aquarium exhibits species from Puget Sound including octopus, sharks, otters, and seals of Puget Sound. You can gaze through an underwater window where schools of fish wheel and turn before your eyes.

Across the street more than 150 steps lead up to the Public Market. There is also an elevator in the parking garage that goes to Western Avenue, on the back side of the Market. See the Pike Place Market Walk, page 55.

Piers 62 and 63 are used for summer concerts on the pier featuring popular entertainers, from the latest stars to old favorites.

As you approach the marina at the Bell Street Pier 66, notice the tall light tower on the end of the pier – a piece of public art. Formerly the office of the Port of Seattle, the pier has been rebuilt and now contains the marina, three restaurants, and the Odyssey Maritime Museum. Walk into the plaza – you'll see children playing in the fish-shaped wading pond. Then climb the stairs to the top of the building and get a close-up view of harbor activity from the free telescopes and benches. (There is an elevator tucked away behind the stairs.) Cruise ships stop at the dock in the summer, providing a beehive of activity when loading and unloading.

Pier 67 is the site of the Edgewater Hotel, built in 1962 for the city's Century 21 World's Fair – the only hotel directly on the waterfront. It used to advertise that guests could fish out their windows and the chef would cook their catch, but no longer. Its other claim to fame is that the Beatles stayed there during their 1960s Seattle tour.

At the Vine Street crosswalk, you may take another one-block detour up Vine Street to see the unusual Community P-Patch on the corner of Elliott Avenue, with its tiled fountain and wrought-iron gates.

Then, back on the waterfront, continue past the stretch of open waterfront, north to Pier 69, the headquarters of the Port of Seattle and the terminal for high-speed Victoria Clipper catamarans to Victoria, B.C. The building's unusual public art revolves around maritime and trade motifs, including a stream that runs the length of the building on the second floor.

The last pier on the waterfront is Pier 70, which was built as a warehouse in 1901 for a fish processor and cannery. Near here the Great Northern Railroad built the first dock for trade to the Orient. At one time there were two 300-foot long docks here, the largest of their kind in the world, accommodating the steamships *Minnesota* and *Dakota,* which carried freight and passengers until shortly before World War I. When containerized cargo ships became the rule in the 1960s, Pier 70 was no longer profitable. In 1970 it was converted to shops and restaurants, becoming the first modern tourist-oriented pier. *Spirit of Puget Sound* cruises depart from the north side of the pier.

You may end your walking tour at Pier 70, or continue on into Myrtle Edwards Park. (See the Myrtle Edwards Park and Elliott Bay Park walk, page 43.)

Return to your car and see the views from the opposite direction. Or hop on one of the colorful Waterfront Streetcars and enjoy the ride back.

NOTES

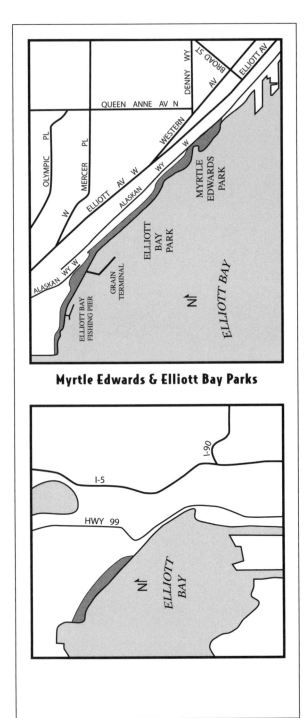

Myrtle Edwards & Elliott Bay Parks

MYRTLE EDWARDS & ELLIOTT BAY PARKS

Distance	3 miles round trip
Time	1 hour
Terrain	Level
Restrooms	By the fishing pier
Food	Snack bar in summer

N orth of Pier 70 a comfortable path starts along the shore, goes past a granite sculpture, changes its name, passes the grain elevator and sheltered fishing stations, winds around Pier 86 and ends at Pier 88. At its south end, it's Myrtle Edwards Park; on the north it's Elliott Bay Park.

Getting There

By Car: From the north, head south on Elliott to Broad Street and turn right to Alaskan Way, cross the railroad tracks and turn right into the parking area. Or, head north along Alaskan Way. The parking area is parking meters on the north side of Pier 70, past the trolley barn.

There is also a parking area at the north end at Elliott Bay Park. Head north on Elliott Avenue from Broad Street. At West Galer

Street turn left at the traffic light, cross the railroad tracks, and bear left until you come to a parking area alongside the Elliott Bay Fishing Pier. You can also find parking off Elliott Avenue between West Bay and West Thomas, just north of the grain elevators.

Restrooms are by the north end, by the fishing piers.

Metro: From downtown to Myrtle Edwards Park, go to Western Avenue and Broad – buses #24 or #33.

For Elliott Bay Park, Metro buses #24 or #33 will take you to First and Bay.

Background

Except for signs marking the beginning of Myrtle Edwards Park as you walk north, and Elliott Bay Park along the way, it's hard to tell that these are two separate parks. It would be simpler if the two parks had the same name, but they don't. The City and the Port developed them, using fill dumped from the construction of Interstate 5. Views of the entire Olympic Mountain range, Blake Island, Alki Point, Harbor Island, the cranes of the Duwamish industrial area, and Mount Rainier are outstanding from the parks in any weather. After dark the lights of the city make jewel-like garlands of light.

At one time the first stop on the Lake Shore and Eastern Railroad was called Interbay, around which a little community sprang up at Smith Cove. The 1903 Olmsted Report recommended waterfront parks along Elliott Bay, and in 1968 the City finally bought the land north of Pier 70 to develop a park. The park path stretches north from Bay Street alongside the shoreline until it becomes Elliott Bay Park, continuing to Pier 88, the old rock-filled pier at Smith Cove.

This is not the park originally meant to be named for popular and influential Myrtle Edwards, who served on the Seattle City Council from 1955 to 1968. The city planned to name the new park at the old gasworks on Lake Union for her, but her family objected because they considered it ugly. They thought this beautiful park was more appropriate. It was so named and developed in 1976.

Money is being raised for a sculpture garden that will fill the area between Alaskan Way and Elliott Avenue, north of Broad Street.

The Walk

Start northward from Pier 70 along the path facing the Magnolia viaduct. Walkways are clearly marked for pedestrians and bicyclists to prevent collisions. Look for the massive three-stone concrete and granite sculpture by Michael Heizer titled *Adjacent, Against, Upon,* given to the city by the Virginia Wright Fund.

Continue walking away from the city on the pleasant level path. You will soon come to a small, formal rose garden with a trellis, stone paths, and variety of hybrid tea roses. The city maintains this well-groomed space alongside the bay. Another point of interest is a small beacon called the Shipmate's Light, erected in 1977 "in honor and memory of seamen lost at sea."

The path swerves around coves that are occasionally littered with debris thrown up over the stone bulkhead by winter storms. Local community groups help maintain the area in an annual beach clean-up. Burlington Northern trains pass nearby – their whistles punctuate the sounds of the waves. Several stopping places have exercise equipment – apparatuses that you can jump over, stretch on, or hang from.

As you continue north, a sign welcomes you to Elliott Bay Park. The Port of Seattle's Grain Terminal fenced-off facility looms large next to the water. Its four-story conveyor belt carries more than four million bushels of grain a year into waiting ships flying flags from all over the world. You can see why local residents were unhappy with the Port's decision to build these monster tanks in front of their views.

Amble, run or stroll along to the end of the path. Cormorants, coots, and a variety of ducks seek shelter from the wind there. The Happy Hooker sells bait and espresso to fishermen and joggers (although with irregular hours) along the artificial reef built for this Elliott Bay pier. A small galvanized steel fisherman casting into the bay, by Buster Simpson, stands on a piling by Pier 86. At Pier 88, the path winds around the harbor next to drydocks on a small protected bay.

Retrace your steps to head back to your car, enjoying the views from the opposite direction.

NOTES

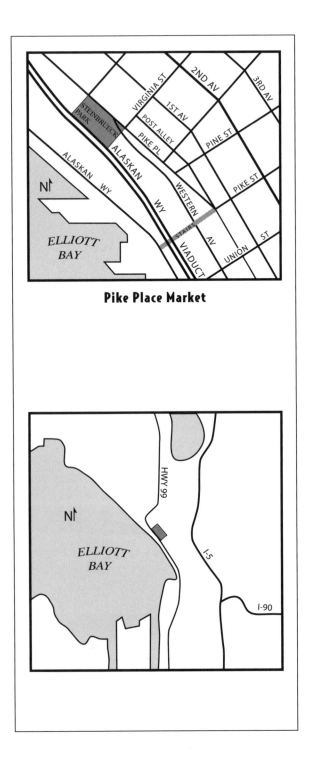

Pike Place Market

PIKE PLACE MARKET

Distance	1 mile
Time	2+ hours
Terrain	Moderate with a hill or two
Restrooms	In Market on the lower level
Food	Restaurants in and around the Market

*A*lmost one hundred years ago the Public Market *started as an open-air market where housewives could buy vegetables and fruit directly from local farmers. With its fabled farmers' tables, flowers, fresh fish, honey and jam, knickknacks, crafts and mysterious treasures it has become a beloved Seattle institution, attracting visitors and locals to its colorful stalls and shops.*

Getting There

By Car: You may get to the Market either from its front side along First Avenue, or from stairs on the back (lower) side along Western Avenue, the area between Virginia and Pike Streets. Parking is difficult in the summer, but some street parking and lots are available on First and Second Avenues, Western Avenue, or under the Alaskan Way Viaduct.

Metro: Buses #15, 18, 21, and 22 stop on First Avenue by the Market. Or take any Metro bus with a stop at Westlake Center (on the street or in the tunnel) and walk west three blocks on Pine Street to Pike Place.

Background

Born from the demands of farmers and house-wives, the Market began as an open air street market on August 11, 1907, and now is the oldest continuously operating farmers' market in the country. The farmers had sold their crops to middlemen who paid them little, then marked up the prices for retail sale. House-wives objected to the high prices they were charged, and farmers complained of being paid too little. After a newspaper campaign, the city council authorized a public farmers' market. Immigrant farmers from the fertile Rainier, Duwamish and White River valleys sold their produce directly to consumers from wagons parked along Pike Place.

The market flourished throughout the 1920s, when Frank Goodwin and Joe Desimone built the shelters and buildings that make up the nine-acre complex. But during World War II the market dwindled when the West Coast Japanese were interned, many of whom were produce farmers, and war jobs attracted workers away from farms. After the war, farm land in the Duwamish and Green River valleys was paved over, and the market's customers migrated to suburban supermarkets. In 1964 the city council approved plans to modernize the market by tearing down most of its buildings and replacing them with office towers, condominiums, and a convention center.

Architect Victor Steinbrueck rallied supporters to save the Market. Calling itself the "Friends of the Market," the group opposed the city's plan and, in 1971, put the issue of market development on the ballot. A majority voted to preserve the market's historic character as the local Market Historical District, which later was added to the National Register of Historic Places. In 1973 the Pike Place Market Preservation and Development Authority, or PDA, was chartered to manage operations. Generous federal urban renewal funds were used to maintain a low-cost food market serving local office workers and the urban poor.

The Market Historical District now includes almost nine acres from First Avenue on the east, Western Avenue on the west, Virginia Street on the north, to the middle of the block between Pike and Union Streets on the south. With increased numbers of tourists and downtown residents in the area, the Market's audience has vastly expanded. The number of farmers and merchants has grown too, and today crafts people vie with farmers and flower growers over available stall space to sell their wares.

Market stalls are either high or low, depending on the kind of goods sold, the rent agreements, and structure of the stall. Traditionally the high stalls, between Pike Street (where *Rachel,* the bronze pig lives) and City Fish, are for permanent vendors who get some of their produce from wholesalers, and the low stalls are made up of day vendors who grow the food themselves. The low stalls offer the best of whatever is in season, from peaches and beets to showy dahlias and lilies. Their location may change from day to day, depending on their place in the Market hierarchy.

If you'd like more history about the Market, stop at the Market Heritage Center, a small building on the west side of Western Avenue, just south of the Desimone staircase.

It has historic photos and videos of Market farmers telling their stories.

The Walk

Note: It's impossible to judge how long this walk might take you, the reader. If you stick to your walking and don't get distracted by the vendors, crowds or restaurants, you could do it in an hour. Or it might take several days. But this is one of the "must do" walks in Seattle. You may prefer to wander randomly through the shops and stalls, but here is a suggested route if you want one. There are two public restrooms in the main market.

Begin your walk beneath the large Market clock and Public Market neon sign on the brick roadway of Pike Place and Pike Street The sign is thought to be one of the oldest neon signs in Seattle, dating from the late 1920s or early 1930s. As you face the water, the Economy Market Building is on your left (the southwest corner of First Avenue and Pike Street). Up its almost hidden stairs there are meeting rooms and the Saints Martha and Mary Chapel for church services. The brick alley below leads to the Market Theatre.

Under the clock lives *Rachel,* the life-sized bronze piggy bank, standing on paving tiles inscribed with the names of donors whose gifts helped save the market. Donations for market projects and human service programs can be put into Rachel. Bronze hoof prints along the sidewalk commemorate recent larger gifts, and really big donors are recognized with bronze fish on the pillars. Inside, fishmongers at Pike Place Fish loudly announce each sale while tossing fresh fish to one another and to customers.

The passageway to the left of the fish market leads you to Place Pigale, once a saloon and now a restaurant with a view. Near the restaurant there is a small public viewing spot where you can look down on the Hillclimb, the Aquarium, and the waterfront. The passageway between Don and Joe's Meats and Market Spice leads to Maximilien's Bistro. Look for a plaque on a post near the meat market with a likeness of George Bartholick, architect for the renovation of the Market.

Facing the Pike Place Fish Market find an arcade where farmers and craft stalls line up to the right and other kinds of businesses to the left with a small Flower Row. To the north is the Main Market – we'll get back to that later.

Take the stairs under the clock down past the rest rooms to the Market Down Under, where you will find four floors of shops with exotic birds, antique jewelry, historic photos, books, magic, and all manner of specialties. Once called the Labyrinth, it was built to provide farmers with protection from bad weather. The stairs also connect to a bridge across Western Avenue, leading down the Hillclimb Corridor to the waterfront past a variety of shops and eating places, one of several accesses to the waterfront. Other stairs and elevators linking the Pike Place Market with the Waterfront below are along Western Avenue and in garages.

Follow the Labyrinth to the north and up the ramp. Real estate developer Frank Goodwin, designed most of the Market's buildings, haphazardly joining the buildings together with uneven ramps and the maze-like layout.

Walk up the ramp, back to the street level and continue north into the Main Market. Enter the stall area, and join the throngs admiring displays of produce, fish and flowers. Garlands of dried red chili peppers and garlic line parts of the ceiling. Crowds swarm around the organic and traditional fruit and vegetable tables, which may include such out-of-the-ordinary items as Maui onions, pomegranates, white fleshed peaches, and hybrid plums. Several families have had the same stalls for generations and take great pride in them.

Just beyond the ramp, in the middle of the main thoroughfare at the foot of Pine Street, you will come to the City Fish Market, a World War I enterprise meant to control fish prices. Continue on to the the "low" or day stalls in the North Arcade, built originally to handle the overflow of produce farmers. From the 1960s on, this area has been reserved for crafts people to sell their work – paintings, photos, honey, jewelry, leather, pottery, T-shirts, and souvenirs. With the Market's present popularity, competition for space is keen as an increasing number of farmers and artists vie for day stall spaces.

The open square area of craft vendors that juts out over Western Avenue overlooking Elliott Bay is Desimone Bridge, named for Joe Desimone, the influential Italian farmer who was spokesman for Market farmers during the 1930s and 1940s. The original bridge leading to the lower Municipal Market was lost in a fire, leaving the "bridge" cut off. Now stairs descend from its northwest corner to Western Avenue below.

Continue north through the main market to open sidewalk where vendors sell crafts from tables. On the west side of Pike Place is Steinbrueck Park, the 1978 tribute to Victor Steinbrueck's dream. Tourists and shoppers can pause, relax, and savor an overlook of the waterfront and Elliott Bay, Alki Point and the Olympic Mountains from this grassy park. Look for two totem poles created by Marvin Oliver, one appropriately topped by two farm-

ers. Parking is available under the park. Politicians and impassioned speakers often address crowds at public rallies here.

Where Western Avenue, Pike Place and Virginia Street meet, turn right and climb Virginia Street to First Avenue, passing the Pike and Virginia Building. Turn right at the Virginia Inn on the corner and begin walking south on First Avenue. Just past the corner of First and Virginia Street see the Butterworth Building, once owned by an undertaker and still containing a crematorium (no longer used) in the basement. Next door, the Alaska Trade Building at one time housed the offices of the Seattle Union Record, the country's only labor-owned newspaper. It published labor leader Anna Louise Strong's call to Seattle workers for a general strike in 1919, the only one in our nation's history. On the corner of First and Stewart is the old Fairmount Hotel, Seattle's first fireproof hotel, built in 1914, now divided into apartments and retail shops. Murals in the lobby show scenes from the early days of the market.

Continue walking south on First Avenue to Stewart Street. Cross Stewart and go down the hill a little way to the cozy courtyard shared by the Inn at the Market and Campagne.

Walk through the courtyard to Pine Street and back uphill to First Avenue. Turn right onto First and go one block to Pike Street, where a fresh flower market occupies the corner. Turn right toward the west, past the 1912 Corner Market Building. Early pictures of the Market show a bustling scene around the Corner Market Building, an attractive three-story building with graceful arches, now containing the flower shop, a community house for seniors, and a variety of other services, as well as restaurants and a cabaret.

Stay right on Pike and turn right onto Pike Place and the Market again, but this time you are going to travel north through narrow Post Alley. Stay on the east side of Pike Place, and keep to the right past Jack's Fish Market into Post Alley at its junction with the Sanitary Public Market. Dairy farmers sold their milk in the Sanitary Market so live animals were kept out to prevent contamination. The Three Girls Creamery is still there. The building burned in a 1941 fire and was rebuilt. In 1981 another remodeling added shops featuring diverse forms of produce, seafood, and a bakery, plus housing upstairs.

Walk north along Post Alley and cross Stewart Street. Stewart House, a renovated 1902 workmen's hotel now used for low income housing, is on the corner. Farther north along Post Alley and Pike Place you will walk past market-rate condominiums. A stairway on the left drops into the small Soames-Dunn courtyard where you may take a break or have a snack. Stay on Post Alley and go past the Champion Building, and the Soames-Dunn Building. In 1918 Dunn's Seeds was only a farm site and Soames Paper Company sold paper bags to market farmers. Today the two have been merged into a stylish structure. Pass a trattoria marked only by its pink door and Kells, an Irish pub. Continue walking north to the Post Alley Market Building, where you can find ethnic specialty gifts. In the basement is a thrift shop with recycled goods for area residents. Pass Upper Post Alley containing the Pike Place Senior Center and the Pike Market Clinic.

Go down hill at Virginia and turn left onto Pike Place to walk back south along the east side of Pike Place along the Soames-Dunn Building. The Starbucks here was the first Starbucks store, recently remodeled. Other shops, Emmett Watson's Oyster Bar, a hardware outlet, a tobacco store, a smokehouse, and a selection of ethnic cafés line the street and are tucked inside. Continue south on Pike Place across Stewart to the Seattle Garden Center, built in 1908 as an egg market and later used as an economy shoe store. Today it offers a selection of herbs, bulbs and flowering plants. A gourmet kitchen shop is above.

Continue walking south on the east side of Pike Place. The old Triangle Market Building, built in 1908, merged with the former Silver Oakum Building, which once housed sailors and merchant seamen. Originally the Triangle Building was where shoppers could choose from a selection of chickens hung from the ceiling. Today your choices are among shops, craft stalls, a bakery, a Greek deli, an upstairs Bolivian restaurant, and apartments.

As you cross Pike again you will be back at the Economy Market. Stop at De Laurenti's for a delicious cheese or sausage pizza, or choose from cheese, salamis and eighteen different kinds of olives. Pick up an out-of-town newspaper at Read All About It to find out what's happening in the world.

Return to your car or bus.

NOTES

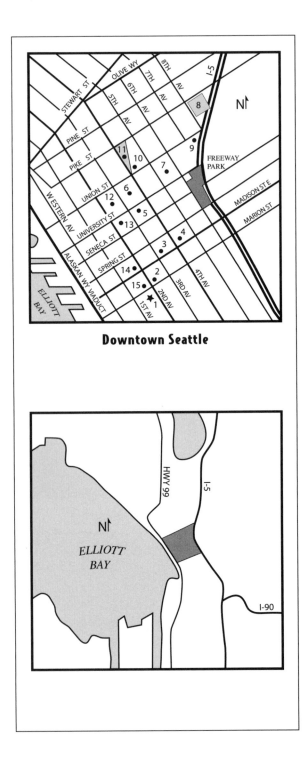

Downtown Seattle

DOWNTOWN

Distance	1 hour
Time	1 mile
Terrain	Level
Restrooms	In public buildings
Food	Restaurants and coffee shops

*S*eattle's downtown is acclaimed for its history and architecture, stunning views and its challenging hills. This walk will show you how to navigate the city without hiking boots.

Getting There

Park in the middle of the city and take any downtown bus to First Avenue and Marion.

Background

Seattle's founding fathers came here at a time when the United States was encouraging settlement in the West by offering land grants of 160 acres a person or 320 a couple. Intrigued by stories that drifted back east about the unknown opportunities in the Northwest, Seattle's first families came to build a city, and had the experience, skills and vision for the task. However, they also had egos, and couldn't agree on how to lay out their hilly town. Doc Maynard and David Denny conformed to the custom of the time and platted their acres in Pioneer Square and Seattle Center, respectively, on a north-south axis, but Arthur Denny, Carson Boren, William Bell and Henry Smith followed the shore line for their plats, creating not only those annoying triangular intersections but the streets running straight up our steep hills.

City engineers have tried to mitigate the problems this created by filling in ravines and sluicing down hills, but we are still left with some challenging hikes through the downtown area. This walk shows a creative way around them.

The Walk

As much of this walk is inside, you might want to save it for a rainy day.

Note: Some office buildings are closed after business hours and on weekends, and Seattle's never-ending construction may close parts of this route from time to time.

Start at First Avenue and Marion Street, at the Exchange Building on the south side of Marion (1). The 1928 Exchange Building is one of the Seattle's most beautiful buildings, designed by John Graham Sr. for the Pacific Stock Exchange. Look at the art-deco brass grill work and the black marble in the First Avenue lobby as you pass through. Take an elevator to the fourth floor, marked 2nd Ave. This is the main lobby, with Belgian marble, more brass trim and a gilt ceiling with art deco motifs. Walk out the front door to Second Avenue, and turn around to admire the front of the building before moving on.

Walk north across Marion Street and find the manhole cover to see a map of the city. You can see where the different claims changed directions. Then cross Second Avenue to the escalators in front of the Wells Fargo bank building (2), designed in 1980s by John Graham Jr. Ride the escalator up all the way to bank's lobby, walk through the lobby to the left and out the front door to Third Avenue. The large *Seattle Tulip* by Tom Wesselmann was the building's contribution to Seattle's 1% for Public Art.

Walk to the corner of Madison and cross kitty corner across Madison to the tall black wall of the 1001 Fourth Avenue Plaza building (3). Find the entrance to escalators in the middle of the building and start up. Keep going on the escalators until you reach the fifth floor, actually the main lobby of the building. Wend your way around to the front of the building, admiring the large *Untitled Painting* by Sam Francis on the front wall, another 1% for Public Art piece. Outside in the plaza is Henry Moore's massive *Three-Piece Sculpture: Vertebrae*. When the building was sold a few years ago the sculpture was sold also and new owners planned to send it to Japan. After a huge public outcry, the sculpture was repurchased and still rests in front of the bank for all to enjoy.

Walk to the corner of Madison and cross Fourth Avenue to the Seattle Public Library (4), soon to be replaced with a new building designed by Rem Koolhaas. Take the escalators up to the top floor and walk out the door to the plaza with one of the early George Tsutakawa fountains, *The Fountain of Wisdom*.

Cross Spring Street. Walk north on Fifth Avenue one block, past the parking garage, to Seneca Street to the Four Seasons Olympic Hotel and down Seneca Street to enter the hotel from the Seneca Street door (5). Go up into its magnificent lobby. The original Territorial University was located here on ten acres donated by Arthur Denny, before moving to its present campus in 1895. Built in 1924 as part of the University of Washington's Metropolitan Tract, the Olympic Four Seasons Hotel is still one of Seattle's grandest hotels.

Go down the escalator and out the parking circle. Cross over University Street in the middle of the block, into the Rainier Tower (6). If you have time, go up to the plaza at the top of the shopping arcade and get a view of the downtown core. Then back down inside the building to the last landing (one flight up from the coffee level). You will see the beginning of a long corridor past the shops. Walk along the tunnel corridor as it passes under the Fifth Avenue Theater, past Eddie Bauer, and under the Hilton Hotel. Look for the large terra cotta Indian head tucked in an alcove, one of the pieces removed when the original buildings were torn down for the Rainier Tower. The walls are covered with photos depicting Seattle's history.

At the end of the tunnel take the escalator up to the lobby between One and Two Union Square. Walk outside (to the left) and see the plaza and waterfall hidden away between the two buildings (7). In the summer free concerts are held here every Thursday under the city's "Out to Lunch" program. Go to the end of the plaza, into Two Union Square and up the broad stairway, or take the escalator on the left. Continue through the lobby and out the doors at the end, into the plaza Two Union Square shares with the Washington State Convention and Trade Center (8). Note the massive gong from Japan.

Turn left and go into the Convention Center. Those nonsensical neon words are another 1% for Public Art, as are the displays throughout the building. Go to the escalators and go up two floors to the fourth floor. Walk out the doors to your left, to the public garden (9). Behind the *Seattle George Monument* by Buster Simpson, a work that morphs the profile of our city's namesake with George Washington's, there are stairs that lead up to Eighth Avenue. Or you may walk through the park to the right as it becomes Freeway Park and go up Spring Street.

You are now on Eighth Avenue, at the foot of First Hill, having negotiated the steepest part of Seattle. You have "climbed" eight blocks and more than 20 stories, without a serious hill.

To go back to First Avenue, go back into the Convention Center, down all the escalators to the Galleria level (the first floor). As you step off the escalator, notice the grand totem pole between the two escalators – there is a plaque at its base telling its history. Then walk past the fountain, out the front door, to Pike Street. Turn left and walk down Pike to Fourth Avenue, to Westlake Park (10), the triangular plaza with the granite pavers. The large pink granite blocks are another 1% for Public Art, representing Seattle's seven hills. Walk north through the park, across Pine Street, into Westlake Center (11). Take the escalator and stairs down to the Metro level and step on a free bus heading south.

Ride to the next stop, University Street, and walk out to Second Avenue (12). In front of Benaroya Hall there is a sheltered park and, below that, a War Memorial Wall with the names of Washingtonians who have died in military actions since the Second World War.

Walk south on Second Avenue, past the Washington Mutual Building, and the broken columns titled *New Archetypes* that fill the plaza (13).

Cross Seneca and pass by the street art by Jack Mackie in front of the bank building, all having to do with money. Cross Second Avenue and cross Spring Street to the Federal Reserve Bank Building (14). There are three pieces of understated art in front of its very cold facade.

Cross Madison Street to the plaza in front of the Federal building (15). The art in the plaza, titled *Landscape of Time,* is by Isamu Noguchi and was one of the first pieces of public art in the 1970s, highly controversial at the time because of its high cost and understated nature.

To finish the walk you may walk down the zig-zagging stairs on the left, which pass by the bronze eagle by Philip McCracken called *Freedom,* or go into the Federal Building to take the elevator down (it's on the left), and you're back where you started.

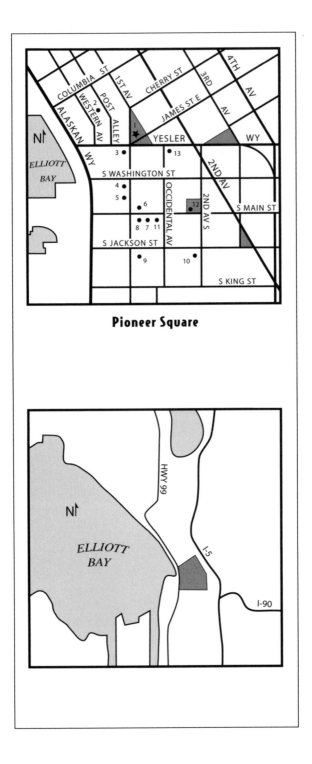

Pioneer Square

PIONEER SQUARE

Distance	1 mile round trip
Time	1 hour or more, depending on your stops
Terrain	Level
Restrooms	In Klondike Gold Rush National Park
Food	Restaurants

Businessmen opened Seattle's first mill, banks and stores along the muddy streets and alleys in Pioneer Square. Now its streets are lined with Victorian street lamps and gracious turn-of-the-century brick and stone buildings, housing cozy shops, galleries, book stores and restaurants, evoking images of early-day Seattle.

Getting There

By Car: From the north, drive south on I-5 and take the James Street exit #168B to the waterfront. Or from downtown Seattle, drive south on First, Second, or Third Avenues.

From the south, take the Safeco Field exit #164A and head toward the water.

Park under the freeway or in one of the many lots near the stadiums.

Metro: Take bus #15, #18, #21, #22, or #56 heading south on First Avenue and get off near Yesler Way. In the Metro tunnel, get off at the Pioneer Square station.

Background

Seattle's pioneer families spent their first winter on Puget Sound at Alki (present-day West Seattle). The following spring (1852) they moved across Elliott Bay to what was then eight acres of dry land surrounded by 1500 acres of mud flats. They built around Elliott Bay's protected deep harbor in spite of nearby steep cliffs, streams fed by fresh water springs, and a lagoon, which complicated the platting of the city.

They soon staked out their donation claims, which at that time were 320 acres for each couple, and settled into their new town. History has called the new immigrants "visionary," but unfortunately they had different visions for the layout of their young city, resulting in our odd alignment of streets and confusing intersections.

Henry Yesler arrived a few months later and built his sawmill on the waterfront at the foot of Mill Street, the present-day Yesler Way. Lumbermen skidded logs from the wooded hills down to Yesler's mill and wharf, so the road became known as Skid Road. Years later, when the business district had moved north, Skid Road became "skid row," a synonym for the down-and-out people who stayed behind.

This was where the life of early Seattle centered. The city's first bank was here, as well as the post office, churches and shops. In 1872 three men were lynched by a mob in this neighborhood, and here in 1886 the Seattle Rifles subdued another mob who wanted to lynch Chinese laborers.

When the Great Seattle Fire of 1889 burned most of downtown's wooden buildings, the city required builders to use brick and stone in new construction to prevent another fire. Business owners in the city's booming business district quickly rebuilt, creating the stately buildings that now fill Pioneer Square. As you walk along you'll notice many buildings have windows below the level of the sidewalk. When these buildings were built after the fire, the city was still at its original level, partly submerged by incoming tides twice a day. After the buildings were built and sewers and water lines installed, dirt from adjacent hillsides filled in the tide flats to the current level and a temporary breakwater wall was installed to stabilize the area.

After World War I many businesses moved north, abandoning the buildings, which fell into decline and disrepair. Missions, shelters, and social service agencies moved in to aid homeless street people. It was not until the 1960s and 1970s that people re-discovered Pioneer Square's neglected buildings and began to restore them. Some had already been destroyed because of a city policy that encouraged parking lots. The grand old buildings you see today were built between 1889 and 1896 in Richardsonian Romanesque style for prosperous businesses and shops. Other buildings in the area were working men's hotels for the mill workers and ship builders, or warehouses for the shipping companies. South of Main Street was the red light district, referred to as "down on the sawdust."

As you walk along you will notice the sidewalks have an odd tilt in many places. Much of the original fill was sawdust from Yesler's mill, which has compacted over the years, leaving the roads lower than the buildings and their sidewalks.

Today Pioneer Square is a Historic District, which encompasses the area between Cherry Street on the north and King Street on the south, Third Avenue on the east, and the waterfront on the west. Area buildings bear the names of early business leaders. There's the Lowman Building named for James Lowman, president of the Yesler Logging Company, the town's biggest business for many years. Judge Cornelius Hanford was the first United States District judge of Washington Territory. The Lowman and Hanford Building is between the Howard Building, in the same style, and the newly restored Denny-Terry building, built as a hotel at the time of the Gold Rush.

Its charm and historic character make Pioneer Square a popular tourist attraction with galleries, shops and restaurants filling the old buildings. New residents, businesses and construction projects planned for nearby buildings will impact the district significantly.

The Walk

Begin at First Avenue and Yesler Way (1) in the triangular Pioneer Place Park. The tall Seattle Totem Pole on the north side is a 1939 replica of a Tlingit pole installed here at what was the heart of the business district. The original pole was stolen by Seattle businessmen from a Tongass village in 1899; this replacement was commissioned as a federal project in the thirties and carved by descendants of the original craftsmen. Typical of many totem, or house, poles, this pole depicts several Indian myths, including the raven trickster who stole the moon and sun. It was dedicated to a woman who was head of the Raven Clan. (See Viola Garfield's *Seattle Totem Poles* for more information.)

The ornate six-story Pioneer Building, built by Henry Yesler, sits on the corner of First and James facing the plaza, the site of his first home. Designed by Elmer Fisher, architect of more than 50 downtown structures, the Pioneer Building was one of the first buildings to go up after the Seattle Fire and is one of the oldest restored buildings in Seattle. With its heavy rounded arches, brick walls, massive stone entrance, and floral and animal terra cotta ornaments, the Pioneer Building is a classic example of the Romanesque Revival style which Fisher introduced to the Northwest. Originally it also had a central tower, which deteriorated and was taken down in the 1930s. Look on the cornerstone for the city's Datum point, from which the heights of buildings and streets were measured. If you would like to complete your above-ground walk with an Underground Tour, you can buy tickets next door.

On the corner, the intricate glass and cast iron pergola provided shelter for streetcar passengers; an elegant restroom below it has been closed for many years. The drinking fountain with the bust of Chief Seattle is one of two sculptures of Seattle's namesake created by James Wehn (the other is at Tilikum Place). The pergola and statues were built for the 1909 World's Fair, known as the Alaska-Yukon-Pacific Exposition (AYP), which was held on the University of Washington campus. (As we write this, the pergola was lying in a heap on the sidewalk, a victim of a passing truck. Plans are to have it restored and put back in its original location.)

From the pergola, cross First Avenue at Yesler to the Mutual Life Building on the northwest corner, an elegant Victorian structure on the site of Henry Yesler's old cookhouse. Peek inside to see the elevator's ornate iron grate.

Continue west on Yesler Way toward the water to see two old hotels, the Post Hotel and the Traveler's Hotel, used by workingmen. Turn right (north) on the first street, Post Alley. Across the street you'll see the back side of the Seattle Steam Corporation Building (2).

Walk to the corner and turn left onto Columbia, crossing Post. You may be able to peek inside the windows of the Journal of Commerce Building and see the original floor with the Journal of Commerce spelled out in its tiles. The building with its rusticated stone base and brick walls has been the home of that publication for over 100 years.

Cross Western Avenue, turn left and head south along Western. Look at the front of the dark Seattle Steam Corporation Building, with its elegant Romanesque windows. The company still provides heat for many downtown buildings. Railroad tracks remain in the street from early days when it was coal fired.

At the corner, cross the street and turn left onto Yesler and return to First Avenue.

If you look east up Yesler Way you will see Seattle's oldest restaurant, the Merchants' Cafe, in continuous operation since just after the 1889 fire. Imagine the changes in customers this place has seen. Seattle's first black resident, Manuel Lopes, is believed to have opened the town's first barber shop near here in 1852.

Another Fisher building, the rusticated stone Yesler Building (3) on the corner of First Avenue and Yesler Way, stands on the site of the original Yesler Hall. President Benjamin Harrison spoke from its balcony to Seattleites when he visited in 1891.

Turn right onto First Avenue and walk south along the west side of First Avenue. Note the City Light manhole cover with a map of

downtown Seattle. You can clearly see where the pioneers disagreed about the streets' orientation. The newly refurbished large red brick Northern Hotel spans several street-level shops. Now called the Terry-Denny Building after Arthur Denny and Charles Terry who built it in 1889, it was a major hotel during the Klondike Gold Rush. The gray brick Maynard Building (4) on the corner of First and Washington sits near the site of the city's first bank. Dexter Horton became the Seattle's first banker when he stored customers' money in a strong box under the floor boards in his store. The story is told that Horton then bought a safe, and when he discovered it had no back he pushed it up against a wall – so no one knew. Later his banking company became the Seattle First National Bank. The stairs to the toy store lead down to the city's original street level. Across the street note the sign on the Delmar Building for the State Hotel, advertising rooms for 75 cents. No rooms are available here for any price today.

From the corner of First Avenue South and Washington Street look down the street to get a glimpse of the waterfront. Option: You may want to walk west on Washington past the St. Charles Hotel and the Washington Park Building (1890) to the waterfront. On Alaskan Way find the Washington Street Boat Landing (1920) where Indians selling salmon and crafts came in their canoes. Later foreign seamen could find a haven. An iron and steel pergola shielded passengers waiting for the ferry. (See Waterfront Tour, page 31.) Return to First Avenue and turn right.

Head south along First to the J&M, a Gold Rush-era bar in the old Schwabacher building (5). Next look for the Central Tavern, another early bar which calls itself the "oldest sec- ond-class tavern." The New England Hotel Building (1889) was once the site of Doc Maynard's first home.

At Main Street, cross First Avenue to the east side. Turn north (left); pass a couple of doorways and enter the Grand Central Hotel Arcade (6) with the glass and metal grill-work doors. Called the Squire-Latimer Building when it was built in 1889, it is another good example of how Seattle changed after the fire. Originally the lower level of this arcade was the street level. Ralph Anderson and a team of local architects restored this handsome build- ing in 1971 – one of the first buildings to be saved in the area. It is now home to a restaurant and shops.

Walk through Grand Central and out the back door to Occidental Park (we'll come back here later). Turn right outside the door and cross Main Street by the Trolley stop to the tiny Klondike Gold Rush National Historical Park, at 117 South Main (7) (look for the flags above the doorway). It is not really a park, but a free one-room museum in a turn-of-the-century building. The exhibits chronicle the gold fever that swept the country in 1897, when the steamer *Portland* docked in Seattle with its legendary ton of gold. Inside you can see demonstrations of gold panning and artifacts from the Klondike, as well as movies. Its location here commemorates the enormous impact the gold rush had on early Seattle. Suppliers of mining equipment and gear made fortunes without ever leaving town. Note: This makes a good restroom stop.

Walk west on Main to the corner of First Avenue South to the Elliott Bay Book Company (8), the former Globe Hotel (1890). One of Seattle's most popular independent book stores, it has a basement cafe lined with books to read while you eat. Its location is the site of Seattle's first hospital, where Doc Maynard's wife Catherine nursed her husband's patients in their home's spare bedrooms. Later, Mary Ann Conklin operated a hotel/bordello named the Conklin House on this site until it burned in the Great Seattle Fire. Nicknamed "Madam Damnable" because of her ferocious temper and foul language, it's said that she intimidated a squad of Marines sent to occupy the hotel during the 1855 Battle of Seattle. Across the street, on the southwest corner of First Avenue South and Main Street, the Bread of Life Mission is housed in the Matilda Winehill Building (1890). Doc Maynard opened his first store here in 1852.

Turn left and walk along First Avenue to South Jackson. Note the small Maude Building across the street, which was once owned by George Carmack, the most successful of the Klondike gold miners.

Cross Jackson, to the Northwest Fine Woodworks Gallery on the corner, in the Wax and Raine Building (9). Turn left and walk east on South Jackson; you will pass by the 1900 Fisher Building with more recent Art Deco terra cotta decoration added to its exterior. It and the neighboring building house galleries displaying art by Northwest artists.

As you walk up South Jackson, look down the side streets and you can admire the new stadium construction. A new Seahawks football stadium is replacing the former Kingdome. Just beyond, the new Safeco Field (the Mariners' baseball stadium) is open to the skies for home games. There are several restaurants catering to sports audiences along King Street and nearby streets.

Continue on Jackson, past the new Metro building on Occidental, to Amtrak's run-down King Street Station on the Second Avenue Extension (10). James J. Hill built the station with its elegant Venetian campanile-style tower for his Great Northern Railroad in 1909. Look to the Union Station across the street, recently restored and incorporated into a new project by Microsoft co-founder Paul Allen. Originally opened in 1911, it served passengers on the Union Pacific and Milwaukee Railroads for sixty years, until Amtrak began using the King Street Station in 1971.

During the day you can walk through Union Station to get to the International District, the center of the Asian and Pacific communities on its east. (See International District tour, page 83.)

Retrace your steps on Jackson back to Occidental (between First and Second Avenues), and cross Jackson to the pedestrian-only Occidental Avenue South Mall. Head north on Occidental. The bank on the southeast corner of Occidental and Main Street (11) is the original site of a blockhouse where pioneer settlers retreated during the day-long Seattle Indian War in 1855 – there's a plaque on the corner of the bank. Today you can walk peacefully down the block past its shops, galleries and cafes. The art galleries of Pioneer Square celebrate openings of new shows with First Thursday Gallery Walks, a free open house on the first Thursday evening of every month. Other times, most are open with regular hours so you may see and purchase new works.

On the Main Street side of Occidental, the Visitor Information booth (open in the summer) once was an elevator cage in the Maynard Building.

Cross Main Street and turn right to the almost hidden Waterfall Garden Park on the corner at Second Avenue and South Main (12). The Casey family founded what became United Parcel Service on this spot in 1907 and built the park in 1977 to honor their employees. Though the enclosed garden with its man-made waterfall cascading over rocks is small, its oasis effect is refreshing and soothing.

Return to Occidental Park. The cobblestoned park displays the Fallen Firefighters Memorial sculpture, which commemorates Seattle's firefighters who have died in the line of duty, a modern glass pergola and recent carved totems.

Walk north through Occidental Park, cross Washington Street and continue on Occidental to Yesler.

On the corner of Yesler and Occidental (13), the Interurban Building is the original location of the Interurban Railway Depot. (The Interurban was a commuters' line running between Bellingham and Olympia, taken out of service after World War II and immortalized in Fremont with the sculpture *Waiting for the Interurban.*) At the corner entrance look for a lion's head ornament.

Look up Yesler Way to see another beloved Seattle landmark, one of its earliest high rise buildings. The white terra cotta Smith Tower, with forty-two stories, was for many years the tallest building west of the Mississippi. Built by L.C. Smith, the "Smith" in Smith-Corona typewriters and Smith and Wesson guns, its distinctive style still stands out, though now dwarfed by higher neighbors. Gilt Indian heads look down from the lobby ceiling at the elaborate copper and brass doors of the hand-operated elevators, unlike any remaining in the city. If it's open you may visit the 35th floor Chinese Temple room and the observation deck circling the base of the pyramidal tower for a fee. On the top, look out over the Pioneer Square community and imagine this area in 1914 when it was new.

Across Second Avenue, the "Sinking Ship Parking Garage," formerly the site of the old Seattle Hotel, is a sad story. The first hotel on the site was the elegant and palatial Occidental Hotel in 1884. It was replaced with the Seattle Hotel a few years later. Rebuilt again after the Great Seattle Fire of 1889, it was torn down in the 1960s because of its dilapidated condition although many citizens felt it should have been protected. Its destruction – and the unattractive garage that replaced it – began the Pioneer Square restoration movement. The Pioneer Square Historic District Association was formed and since then has helped to encourage the saving and restoring of other old buildings. Look up at the garage/ship from Yesler Avenue and the appropriateness of its nickname will be clear.

Return to your car or bus stop.

NOTES

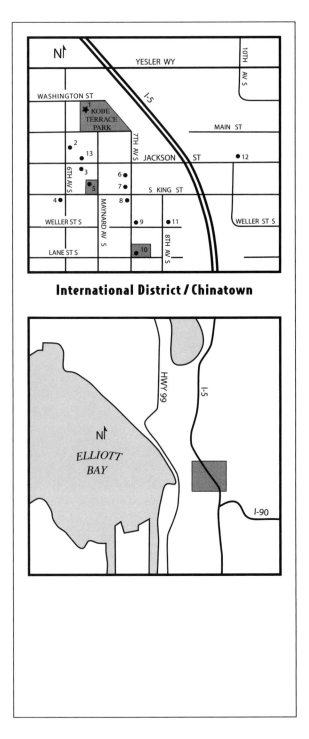

International District / Chinatown

INTERNATIONAL DISTRICT/ CHINATOWN

Distance	1½ miles
Time	2 hours
Terrain	Mostly moderate, with one major hill
Restrooms	Sanicans
Food	Restaurants

A sian immigrants, looking for a better life in the U.S., helped build the Northwest in the nineteenth century. A walk through the International District offers a glimpse into many Asian cultures and the roles they have played in our area's development.

Getting There

By Car: From the north: Take I-5 to exit 165A (James Street). Follow Sixth Avenue straight ahead, across Yesler, to South Washington Street. Park on the street or in parking lots on Washington or Main. Or, from downtown, drive south on Fifth Avenue to South Jackson Street.

From the south: Take I-5 to exit #164 (Dearborn). Turn left onto Fifth Avenue, and go to Jackson Street. Turn right onto Jackson; turn left onto either Seventh Avenue or

Maynard and park along the street or in a lot.

Metro: The Metro bus tunnel has an exit in the International District, and routes #7, #14, and #36 serve the area on surface streets. The Waterfront Streetcar goes to the edge of the area at Fifth Avenue. Unfortunately, no matter what you do, you'll have a hill either at the beginning or the end of the walk.

Background

A few years after the pioneers had settled in the Northwest, immigrants from Asia arrived. They helped build the new West Coast towns and the railroads that tied them together. Many settled in the International District, which, like neighboring Pioneer Square, is an Historic District, where most buildings date from the turn of the century.

Seattle's original Chinatown was near Second Avenue and South Washington Street on filled-in tide flats. Young Chinese men had come to California in the 1860s hoping to find gold in the "Gi Gun San" – the "Old Mountain of Gold." When that didn't pan out, many came by steamship to the Northwest's new port city for jobs in logging camps, salmon canneries and railroad construction. Work became scarce when the railroads were completed, and, as competition for jobs increased, anti-Chinese sentiment grew. The federal Chinese Exclusion Act of 1882 banned Chinese from owning property. Anti-Chinese sentiments peaked locally in 1886 when rioters forced most of the 350 Chinese living in the Puget Sound area out of town. Only a few remained hidden in the International District.

The community gradually grew again, and by 1889 a second Chinatown near the northeast corner of Second Avenue and Main Street had been built. Again immigrant Chinese provided labor for railroads, canneries, farms, and labor agents; importers, retailers and owners of residential hotels flourished despite prejudice. Chinatown developed a merchant elite that ran the Chinese Benevolent Association, the governing body that maintained the Chinese school, policed the community, and assisted new immigrants. The Exclusion Act was finally repealed in 1943, but the national quota still limited Chinese immigrants to 50 annually.

Japanese immigrants began to arrive and take over some Chinese homes and jobs before the end of the nineteenth century. Since the United States was developing trade with Japan at this time, it was decided at first that the 1882 Chinese Exclusion Act did not apply to Japanese. The first Japanese, the Issei, were mainly unskilled farm laborers; others worked in coal mines east of Lake Washington, as well as lumber mills, canneries, and sawmills, hoping to return home rich. They built a Nihonmachi, or Japantown, near Main Street, north of the second Chinatown. Although laws prohibited the Issei from owning land, some Japanese ran truck farms in the fertile Rainier Valley where they eventually supplied 75 percent of the produce for Seattle and the Pike Place Market. Japanese businessmen opened stores, restaurants, and residential hotels near Main and Jackson streets.

The Klondike Gold Rush of the 1890s brought more Asian immigrants, and in 1897 the Great Northern Railway Company began actively recruiting Japanese to build tracks. New shops, hotels, restaurants, and boarding houses opened in the International District.

By 1900 the Japanese-American community reached from Fifth to Tenth avenues, between Main and Dearborn streets, and was Seattle's largest minority population; by 1910

Seattle had more than 6,000 Japanese. Japanese restaurants, barbershops, pool halls, and cafes lined Main and Jackson streets. Nippon Kan, the Japanese Hall, filled with dance, music, and drama programs. Seattle's Nissei (second generation Japanese) lawyers, doctors, dentists, photographers, plumbers, and electricians advertised in three daily Japanese-language newspapers in the early 1920s.

In 1924 Congress voted to apply the Exclusion Act to Japanese after all, denying them entry into the country. Japanese had never been eligible for naturalization or citizenship and state laws prohibited them from owning land. The bombing of Pearl Harbor in 1941 created major problems for Japanese-Americans. President Roosevelt's 1942 edict, Executive Order #9066, sent 112,000 West Coast Japanese, including 7,000 from Seattle, to internment camps, requiring them to forfeit their businesses and personal property.

Before the war Japanese had operated 80 percent of the hotels, restaurants, groceries, laundry/dye works, importers, barber shops, law offices and dental clinics in the blocks between Sixth Avenue and South Main. Most of the buildings in which these businesses were housed have been torn down and replaced with parking lots and low income senior housing. During the Japanese internment the city demolished Nihonmachi north of the present I-5 and later built Yesler Terrace, one of the first integrated public housing projects in the U.S., in its place.

After the war Nihonmachi was a ghost town, lacking the vitality to recover. Many Japanese sold their businesses, retired or moved away. Others were taken over by second generation Japanese or were bought by Chinese. Local housing was scarce so the Japanese who returned relocated throughout the city and suburbs. They did not receive citizenship rights until 1952; most of their property losses were never compensated. A federal reparation payment finally came in 1996, too late for most.

In the 1920s Filipinos became the third Asian group to settle in Seattle in large numbers. Because the United States had acquired the Philippines from Spain in the Spanish-American War Filipinos were able to immigrate as American nationals, rather than as foreigners. The Japanese American Courier announced that a "New Manila" had situated itself alongside "Chinatown" and "Little Tokyo." Filipino immigrants soon discovered what Chinese and Japanese had learned: American growers and canneries might want their labor, but American workers resented them. By 1930 Seattle was a major port of entry for Filipinos and had the third largest Filipino population in the United States, with the Philippine and Eastern Trading Company on Fifth Avenue by far their largest Seattle business. The vast majority became farm laborers, migrating from hop fields to apple orchards, then to canneries, through the seasons. In 1934 a congressional act made Filipinos aliens and allowed resentful local Seattleites to impose a quota of fifty immigrants a year.

Along with changes within the community, other changes from outside affected the Asian community. Following the Jackson Street regrade in 1910, merchants shifted their businesses to the newly paved King Street area, and after the King Street and Union Pacific railroad stations opened, other changes occurred. With the loss of Japanese residents and their community during world War II the International District became home to the elderly, the poor and some transient black workers.

In the 1960s the freeway cut though the International District, splitting it, and by the 1970s, over half of the area's old hotels had shut down and many longtime businesses had moved out. The building of the Kingdome on the western edge threatened the District's survival with traffic congestion and land speculation. The Asian community rallied and bargained with the City Council for compensations such as low income housing, daycare, a community center and garden, and a public association to preserve and renovate historic buildings.

Today there are strong Japanese and Chinese businesses in Seattle. With an influx of South East Asian immigrants in the 1980s after the war in Viet Nam, the District has expanded and moved east of the freeway with renewed vitality. Within the district certain blocks belong primarily to certain ethnic groups. Broadly speaking, proceeding uphill from west to east along Jackson Street starting at Fifth Avenue South, the Japanese and Chinese own the shops in the lower part of the historic area, followed by the Filipinos, Laotians, Thai and Vietnamese east of I-5.

Visit in February before the Chinese New Year celebration or during other traditional holidays when streets are crammed with festivals, dancers, or shoppers buying supplies.

The Walk

Begin your walk at its highest point at the top of South Washington Street at the Nippon Kan Theatre (630 So. Washington Street) and Kobe Terrace Park (1). Built in 1909, the Nippon Kan Theatre was a cultural center for Japanese immigrants. Restored in 1978 the theater is now privately owned and used for events such as judo and kendo competitions, flower displays, art shows, kabuki, and community events. It is on the National Historic Register.

When I-5 was built it divided the Yesler Terrace community and left the small triangle on the west side, which became Yesler Park. Renamed Kobe Terrace Park in the 1970s as part of Seattle's Sister Cities program, the park contains plaques in both Japanese and English about the good will between Seattle and its sister city, Kobe. Kobe donated the prominent 200-year-old Yukimidoro *Snow Viewing Lantern* stone lantern and surrounding cherry trees. On a clear day this high point offers stunning views of Mount Rainier and an overview of the International District. Look across to the imposing building at the top of Beacon Hill, originally built as the Marine Hospital, which became the Pacific Medical Center. It was recently bought by Amazon. com.

Make your way down through the one-acre Danny Woo International District Community Gardens on its paths and steps. Depending on the season you might see elderly residents cultivating their small terraced gardens containing traditional Asian fruits and vegetables. You can also walk around the park and down the hill on Maynard – both routes offer outlooks over the south end of the city.

Turn right onto Main Street at the bottom of the garden and walk past the Panama Hotel at 605 South Main on your left. Personal belongings of some of the Japanese who were sent to internment camps are stored in the basement, still waiting for owners to claim them.

Turn left onto Sixth Avenue. The locked iron door leads to a former public bathhouse in the Panama Hotel's basement. Japanese immigrants who lived in hotels preferred public baths and found spiritual regeneration in public bathing. At one time there were six public bathhouses in the International District, but this is the only one remaining.

Continue downhill on Sixth Avenue. On the south wall of the N-P (Northern Pacific) Hotel at 306 Sixth Avenue South (2) is an old painted vertical sign advertising rooms for 50 cents and up. If the door is unlocked, walk into the lobby to view the permanent exhibit of photos of historic Japantown. A particularly haunting photograph is of the Higo Variety Store boarded up during the internment camp years. The hotel was an early residential and commercial cornerstone of pre-World War II Japan Town, a first class hotel. It has been restored with the first floor retaining the old configuration and the upper floors offering low-income subsidized housing. Across the street, the restored wooden building is the Main Street School Annex. Built in 1873, it was the second public school in Seattle and played a major role in the Asian community, serving as the education center for second-generation Asian Americans. The building now houses professional offices and is one of the oldest existing public buildings in Seattle. The white terra cotta building on the corner of Sixth Avenue and Jackson was once the Japanese Chamber of Commerce.

Cross Jackson. The United Savings and Loan Bank on the corner of Jackson and Sixth Avenue (3) was the nation's first Asian American-owned savings and loan association. Its founders, the Chinns, opened the bank to help Asian families who had trouble getting loans from other lending institutions. Note the historic mural of *The Eight Immortals* at the entry, painted by Fay Chong.

Continue on for two blocks on Sixth Avenue to another community icon, Uwajimaya, which fills the west side of the block between

South Weller and Lane streets (4). It is a vast market with Asian food and merchandise, a kind of Japanese supermarket that includes delicacies and specialties of the local community. Fea-turing a cooking school, sushi bar and deli, it also houses the largest Japanese book store in the Northwest. Lacquerware dishes and vases, many glazed in tones of blue and white or celadon green fill the shelves of the gift shop. It has expanded recently and covers more than two blocks – South Weller and Lane Streets – and includes housing. Allow time to go inside for a visit.

Walk up Weller to Maynard and turn left on Maynard. Walk to the corner of South King Street, past the recently renovated Eastern Hotel on the east side, which has photographs and a large mural depicting Filipino life in Seattle. Built at the time of the Jackson Street regrade, it is a fine example of an early multistory apartment hotel in the International District. Its fine brick work has been cleaned in a recent renovation. The building is on both the National Registry of Historic Places and the Seattle Landmarks list.

Cross King Street to Hing Hay Park (5). Often a staging area for events, this park is a community focal point. Look for the dragon mural by John Woo on the back wall of the Bush-Asia Center and the red tile-roofed Grand Pavilion given by our sister city, Taipei. Look also for a memorial to the ten Chinese Americans who died in World War II.

Past Hing Hay Park, the Bush-Asia Center, built in 1915 as a first class hotel to serve railroad passengers, was leased by the Japanese in the 1920s to provide a social hall for receptions. Today it has been rehabilitated into low income residential units. An open air produce market frequently operates at the corner of Jackson and Maynard. Eager shoppers can select fresh Asian vegetables and fruits from crates on the sidewalk.

Across the street the 14-foot bronze sculpture, *Heaven, Man and Earth* by Seattle sculptor George Tsutakawa portrays the totemic forces as stylized characters designed like cairns piled in Tibetan fields.

Turn right at Jackson and walk to Seventh Avenue and turn right at the corner. Just past the corner is the Wing Luke Museum at 407 Seventh Avenue South (6). Named for the first Chinese American elected to the Seattle City Council, this is the nation's only museum preserving the entire spectrum of Asian American cultures. Rather than showing traditional Asian art and history, the museum illustrates the experience, culture and lives of early Asian immigrants to the Pacific Northwest and their contributions to it. Its permanent exhibit titled "One Song, Many Voices" includes donations of diaries, photographs and artifacts from local residents.

The Northwest Asian American Theatre next door is one of only six Asian American theaters in the country. It presents the works of Asian American artists in a performing arts center.

Next, continue walking south past the Milwaukee Hotel (7) on the corner. In 1911 when it was built to house visitors after the Alaska-Yukon-Pacific Exposition it was the largest hotel in Chinatown. Its builder Goon Dip served as Seattle's first Chinese Consul at the turn of the century and had his residence on the top floor. His name appears above the building's doorway on King Street.

Stay on Seventh Avenue and cross King Street.

Just past the corner on the right-hand side, be sure to view the Chinese Community Bulletin Board (8), listed on the official City of Seattle Landmarks list. In the 1960s when it was installed, there were no Chinese language newspapers and it posted notices of news and events for the community. It still does. Since then, a community newspaper has begun publication. Though there were once three daily Japanese papers, the Chinese community had none until 1982, when Assunta Ng, a young Hong Kong immigrant, started the *Seattle Chinese Post*, now called the *Northwest Asian Weekly*. Community news and stories are reported in both Chinese and English editions. Across the street is the ornate China Gate restaurant, originally built as an opera house. On the corner of Weller, the Buddhist Girls School with traditional columns was where Chinese girls took their Chinese language lessons after regular school. It continues to have community classes and functions to this day. Cross the street to the Buddhist Girls School (9) and look back to see the balcony of the Gee Haw Tin building where you were standing and notice how it's been restored.

Continue walking south on Seventh Avenue to Lane Street to the International Children's Park on the corner (10). Families delight in the imaginative bronze dragon designed by Gerard Tsutakawa, a swinging Chinese bridge to cross, and an umbrella rain shelter inside a quiet garden. During cherry blossom season the park grounds are covered with the soft pink snow of cherry petals.

Retrace your steps back to Weller and turn right. Walk up Weller one block, past the playground with the children's murals, to Eighth Avenue South. Turn left and continue north on Eighth Avenue South to the corner of King for the Tsue Chong Noodle Factory, also known as the Rose Brand Fortune Cookie Factory (11). The owners give tours only to school children, but you can walk into the shop at the next corner (King Street) and buy a bag of "unfortunate flats," or failed fortune cookies.

Continue north to reach Jackson once again. As you turn right on Jackson and walk under the freeway through the brightly red and yellow columns with fanciful fish designs you are leaving the Historic District. New businesses east of the freeway catering to the South East Asian community have opened in recent years. Several cafes feature "Pho," a favorite Vietnamese noodle soup. The plain exteriors belie the jumbled assortments of goods and foods inside.

In the next block beyond, at Tenth Avenue South and Jackson (12), look for a combined grocery and pharmacy, the Viet-Wah. The name represents the combination of Vietnamese and Chinese markets. This pharmacy is typically Asian in that it offers a variety of dried sea creatures, such as seahorses and sharkfins, along with dried mushrooms, ginseng, red dates and dried plums, all of which are to be boiled and made into a drink or infused with alcohol. Specific medicinal properties are attributed to each. The pharmacist listens to your symptoms, then prescribes what you need and grinds it up for you.

Rare and exotic fresh fruits and vegetables are displayed alongside those you would find in any supermarket, and are reasonably priced. One day when we were there, Malaysians and Filipinos were buying durians, a deeply incised melon some call "stinky fruit," Polynesians were eyeing taro and casaba, Chinese were buying long beans, thin purple eggplant, white radishes, and bok choy, and everyone wanted pieces of winter melon for their New Year's soup.

A whole case is devoted to different forms of tofu – mild, medium, firm, and pressed into curds. The seafood tanks are a sensory assault. No fish or crustacean is wrapped. Oysters, crabs, and lobsters are alive, and the huge carp, squid, pomfret, catfish, pike, and octopus are freshly killed and often lie in their own blood. In the meat section the beef, pork and chicken portions look like cuts you expect to see, but along with them are more entrails, and bones. Duck is a popular choice for New Year's feasting and are sold with necks, heads, and bills still attached. In other markets whole Peking ducks hang in the windows, already prepared, with their skins dark red-brown and crisp.

Retrace your steps down Jackson. As you return to your car, you may want to succumb to the inviting aromas from the restaurants and bakeries along the way or pick up something at the Higo Variety Store (13). Located just before the corner of Sixth Avenue, Higo is a mini-department store featuring a wide variety of items from teapots and rice cookers, brocade pajamas and chopsticks, to tourist souvenirs. Opened in 1910, it is one of the oldest continuing businesses of Nihonmachi. Aya and Masiko Murakami, daughters of the original owner, worked there all their lives.

Benevolent Associations

Benevolent Associations or tongs line the streets. Look at the tops of buildings to find them. Many have ornate painted balconies, exotic cornices atop buildings, and light posts with pagoda lanterns. Inside, most have an individual shrine and club room. They serve as social clubs, teaching language and citizenship, mediating disputes and as a unifying voice for Chinese family groups, and have a historic reputation as gambling dens. Members gather to play bingo and mah jong.

The Chong Wa Benevolent Association at 522 Seventh Avenue South, housed in a two-story brick building built in 1929, is both a benevolent association and a school. The largest Chinese family association in the District is across the street at 513 Seventh Avenue South, the Gee How Oak Tim Family Association and Hotel. The association had to become non-profit to qualify for federal funds to renovate this building so it now is open to the public. On South Jackson and Seventh Avenue South look for such other examples: The Bin Kung Association at 704 South King, which serves jointly as a Masonic hall, also has a distinctive balcony near the top of the building.

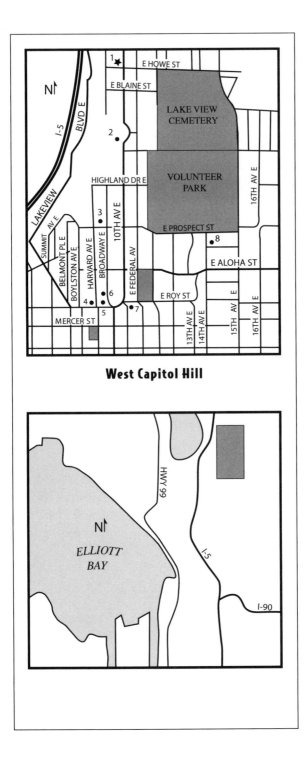

West Capitol Hill

WEST CAPITOL HILL

Distance	3 miles round trip
Time	1½ – 2 hours
Terrain	Variable terrain
Restrooms	No
Food	Restaurants on Broadway

*L*ittle *has changed in this neighborhood since early entrepreneurs, gold rush tycoons, and railroad and timber barons built their mansions and gracious homes here one hundred years ago. Schools, churches, and meeting halls reflect the cultural and artistic aspirations of young Seattle as it settled in and began to mature.*

Getting There

By Car: From I-5 heading south, take the Roanoke exit (#168A), turn left across the freeway and turn right onto 10th Avenue.

From I-5 heading north, take the Lakeview Boulevard exit. Head north from the stop sign, continuing north as the road goes uphill and becomes Harvard. Turn right on Boston, up the hill. Turn right onto Tenth

Avenue East. Park along neighborhood streets between Newton and Howe.

Metro: Bus #7, #9 or #25.

Background

Developer James A. Moore is generally credited with naming Capitol Hill, although historians debate his motives. It's thought he named it after an area in Denver where he grew up, but he may have hoped to entice the state capitol to the area even though its location had already been settled in Olympia. In the 1880s large lots on the hill contained vegetable gardens with picket fences, fruit trees, and elevated plank sidewalks. Streets at first were uneven stump-strewn paths, but were later straightened and graded. James Moore platted his addition soon after the turn of the century, and the surrounding neighborhood became known as Capitol Hill. The land, which had been logged and clear-cut, included the area from Volunteer Park to Howell Street.

Arthur Denny began platting the future Capitol Hill for residences as early as 1861. In 1876 the city bought 40 acres for a planned city park. The mostly undeveloped park served briefly as a city cemetery. After the turn of the century the park was renamed Volunteer Park and the Olmsted Brothers firm created its formal design to fit in with the upper class neighborhood. (See Volunteer Park walk, page 109.)

By 1908 Capitol Hill had become one of the most fashionable residential districts in the city, filled with grand mansions of newly rich lumber men, bankers, shipping magnates, and those who had struck gold in the Klondike. For a short time a fence at Roy Street on Fourteenth Avenue closed off Millionaires' Row and emphasized the neighborhood's exclusiveness. Elegant apartment buildings in Tudor, Norman, and Mediterranean styles from that time still stand along tree-lined streets.

The Walk

The Capitol Hill area is bounded by Interstate 5 on the west, Boyer Avenue on the northeast, and merges with First Hill around Pike Street on the south. We've divided the Capitol Hill walk into two parts, East and West Capitol Hill. Also in the Capitol Hill area are the Lake View Cemetery and Volunteer Park walks. You can do the walks separately as written, or combine parts from one to another for an extended walk.

Begin your walk at the corner of Tenth Avenue East and East Howe (1) with the elegant white terra cotta Rhodes Mansion. Built by Albert Rhodes in 1911 in the style of an eighteenth century Italian villa and hedged with weeping Atlas cedar trees, it has an unobstructed view west over Lake Union to Queen Anne Hill.

Option: Descend the stairs down the hill past secluded gardens and view homes. Turn left and proceed to the street end, dropping down to tree-lined Lakeview Boulevard. Turn left on Lakeview and walk one block south to East Blaine for another set of steep stairs leading back up to Tenth Avenue, pausing to admire Lake Union, the gardens, and to catch your breath.

Head south on Tenth Avenue East along the bend in the road to 1551 Tenth Avenue East, the Episcopal Diocesan House, known as the Leary House. John Leary started this house in 1903 for his wife, Eliza Ferry Leary, daughter of Washington state's first governor, but he died before it was finished. His widow went on to complete the fourteen-room Tudor mansion using the finest craftsmen of the time.

Alfred Bodley was the architect, the Olmsted Brothers firm designed the landscaping, and Louis Tiffany crafted the stained-glass windows and lampshades. It has served as headquarters for the Episcopal Diocese of Olympia since 1948 and is listed on the Seattle and National Registers of Historic Places, as are the two houses to the south. Regular tours are not provided, but during weekdays you are welcome to walk in on the main floor and to look around.

Next door, the house at 1229 Tenth Avenue East was built in 1907 by the Pierre P. Ferry family and, though now a private residence, it was for many years the home of the presiding dean of St. Mark's Cathedral and is it still referred to as the Dean's House. It is also listed on the Seattle Register of Historic Places.

The red brick building between the Deanery and the Cathedral belongs to the Cornish School, a private arts college we'll see later. Originally built for the St. Nicholas School for Girls, the school building was sold in the early 1980s after St. Nicholas merged with the Lakeside School.

Next door is Saint Mark's Cathedral (2), one of Seattle's two cathedrals. Walk inside this enormous neo-Byzantine building, which was started in the 1920s. It was barely roofed before the Great Depression hit and the church went into bankruptcy, leaving the bare concrete walls exposed for sixty years. During World War II the building served as a barracks for U.S. troops. After the war ended the congregation bought their cathedral back. A recent remodel has added brick to the eastern exterior, a new copper roof, and an enormous abstract rose window on its west side.

At Halloween St. Marks has a tradition of showing the silent films, *The Hunchback of*

Notre Dame or *Phantom* to the community. Sunday evening compline services at 9:30 P.M. offer a great chance to visit this cathedral, listen to its mighty Flentrop pipe organ, and hear the men's choir chanting plainsong. In the darkness the cathedral becomes almost medieval.

Continue walking south along Tenth Avenue past the church gift shop and preschool. Turn right on East Highland Drive.

To get an overview of the Harvard-Belmont Historic District, cross the street and walk along the deck of the Scottish Rite Temple. This neighborhood is listed on the Seattle Landmarks Register and on the National Register of Historic Places, the only neighborhood listing. It includes most of the houses between Harvard and Belmont, from East Highland to East Roy street. Some eighty residences and four open spaces are included in the protected area, which also encompasses streets, landscapes, driveways, retaining walls and street lights. Most of these elegant mansions with landscaped gardens and sweeping views were built between 1905 and 1910 for the city's turn-of-the century wealthy businessmen. Garages and carriage houses on

Boylston and Summit today are owned today by a more diverse group.

Across the street, on the north side of Highland Drive, is Samuel Hill's 1909 reinforced concrete mansion at 814 E. Highland (3). Hill, the son-in-law of James J. Hill, the founder of the Great Northern Railroad, built this impressive home at the time of the Alaska-Yukon-Pacific Exposition for his wife, who did not want to live in Seattle. He received many world leaders there, although his wife moved out soon after it was completed. Inside there's a secret passageway and a grand wine cellar. If the sun is out you can set your watch by the sundial on the corner of the house.

Walk west down Highland into the Harvard-Belmont Historic District. You can turn left and walk straight along Harvard for a shorter walk, or zigzag along Boylston, Belmont and Summit avenues through the area for a more extensive tour past these elegant homes. Some particularly beautiful examples are the former Episcopal bishop's house at 1147 Harvard Avenue East, modeled on a famous manor in England, and the gray shingled country house at 1137 Harvard Avenue East, built by lumberman J. H. Bloedel. On the corner of Aloha, the Merrill Court townhouses were built in the 1980s, adjacent to the 1919 gray stucco house. You'll see turn-of-century architectural styles such as Tudor, Gothic Revival, Craftsman, Georgian, Federal, and Mediterranean Renaissance, surrounded by fine old trees and landscaping.

Continue south to East Roy Street and Harvard. (If you took the longer loop, you will walk uphill to Harvard.)

On the corner of East Roy and Harvard is the tan stucco Cornish School of Allied Arts (4). Nellie Cornish founded the school to provide an arts education for children of the new gentry. Patrons contributed so generously that she was able to build this Mediterranean-style building seven years after starting the school. She believed in the inter-relatedness of the arts, including all branches of music, drama, the visual arts and dance. In addition to educating students, she gave opportunities to teachers whose work she admired: Composer John Cage; dancer Merce Cunningham; and theater directors Burton and Florence James. Painter Mark Tobey was on the faculty before he was known, and Martha Graham taught dance. Known affectionately as Miss Aunt Nellie, for years she offered scholarships from her own funds to talented students, many of whom went on to receive national attention. The school continues in the same tradition today as an accredited college.

Cross Harvard Avenue to the east to the Daughters of the American Revolution House (5). Built in 1925 by the Rainier Chapter, the classic white Colonial building's exterior is a replica of George Washington's home at Mount Vernon; its interior is furnished with elegant antiques. Membership is open to descendants of veterans of the War for Independence. The building is rented out for special events and is usually not open to the public.

Across East Roy is the Harvard Exit Theater, originally the Women's Century Club – you can see the name above the doorway. Founded in 1891 by a group of women to prepare for women's participation in the twentieth century, members helped to found the city's first kindergarten and the first public library. Carrie Chapman Catt, the club's first president, was later a nationally famous suffragist. In 1896 the club hosted a reception for Susan B. Anthony; it also successfully campaigned to elect

Bertha Landes as Seattle's first, and only, woman mayor. The club sold the building in 1968 with the provision that members could continue to use it for meetings. It still awards scholarships to local recipients with funds from the building's sale.

Continue up East Roy.

Next door you come to the Loveless Studio Building (6) built in the 1920s and 1930s. On the street level, the small shops have eclectic merchandise, while the apartments above share a private courtyard. If you are lucky the courtyard gate between shops may be unlocked and you can peek inside.

Cross Broadway at the light, walk north around the gas station and head east uphill on East Roy for a block to reach Federal Avenue.

The brick apartments at 1005 and 1014 East Roy Street (7) are Anhalt buildings and are listed on the Seattle Register of Historic Places. Builder Frederick Anhalt's style, with steeply pitched roofs, turrets with pointed tops, mullioned windows, and landscaped courtyards, inspired by the village architecture of Normandy and England, was a unique look for Seattle and much admired. Look for replicas of chateaus, manor houses with terra cotta trim, leaded-glass windows, and, on the roofs, English chimney pots. His beautiful small apartment buildings are tucked in throughout Capitol Hill.

At this point you can turn north on Federal and return to your car. Or cross Federal and continue uphill on the path by the school. Continue on to Thirteenth Avenue. Turn right onto Thirteenth, with its mixture of large new homes, a Japanese-style bungalow and the historic Maryland Apartment building. At Mercer, turn left and go up one more block, to Fourteenth Avenue, James Moore's original development, which was known as Million-aires' Row.

Walk north along Fourteenth Avenue, past some of the grandest, most ostentatious old homes in the city, vestiges of a time when Seattle was young and its new millionaires wanted their homes to reflect the age and dignity of eastern and continental styles. Some have been converted to other uses, such as the Shafer Bailie Mansion Bed and Breakfast and a large old Victorian home, now the headquarters of the United Church of Christ, while many are being renovated by new inhabitants. On the corner of East Prospect the white classical Parker Mansion faces the entrance to Volunteer Park (8). Built in 1909 by George Parker, Seattle's "wireless man," in neo-classical style with Corinthian columns, it has sixteen rooms, five roofed porches, twelve bedrooms, five bathrooms, and seven fireplaces.

If you want to continue through Volunteer Park, see Volunteer Park walk, page 109.

Or, to end your walk, turn left and walk down Prospect to Federal Avenue. Turn right onto Federal Avenue to see the more modest homes of the upper class, beautifully maintained and landscaped. At the east end, the house at 1642 Federal was the home of Dr. Richard Fuller and his mother, who donated the Art Museum to Seattle. Federal is one block east of Tenth Avenue, where we started.

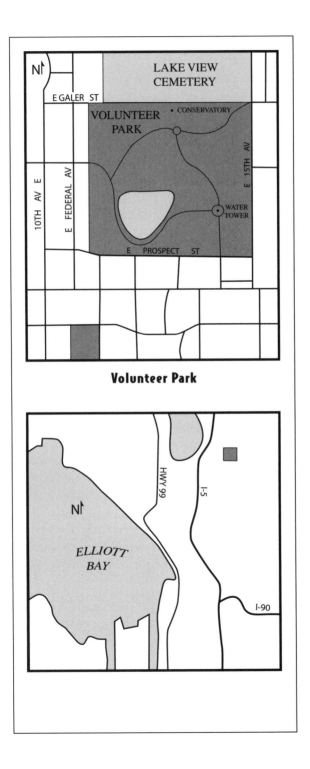

Volunteer Park

VOLUNTEER PARK

Distance	2 miles round trip
Time	1-2 hours
Terrain	Moderate
Restrooms	Yes
Food	No

At the turn of the twentieth century the "City Beautiful" movement was in full flower and Seattle was booming. The most elegant of the Olmsted parks, Volunteer Park, with its gracious curved walkways, organized plantings and spectacular views, remains much the same as its original design.

Getting There

By Car: From I-5 heading south, take the Roanoke exit (#168A), turn left across the freeway and turn right onto Tenth Avenue. At the traffic light at Boston, turn left and follow Boston as it curves around and becomes Fifteenth Avenue. Turn right into the park just past Galer Street.

From I-5 heading north, take the Lakeview Boulevard exit. Turn left at the stop sign and head north. Continue straight, up the hill, as the road becomes Harvard. Turn right on Boston, up the hill to the traffic light. Stay on Boston as it curves around and becomes Fifteenth Avenue. Turn right into the cemetery just past Galer Street.

Park your car on Fifteenth Avenue East or East Prospect near entrances to Volunteer Park or in the park.

Metro: Take a #10 bus to the stop on Fifteenth Avenue East and East Galer.

Background

Note: This walk may be done separately or combined with Lake View Cemetery or either Capitol Hill walk: East Capitol Hill and West Capitol Hill.

It took a long time for Seattle to grow from a small timber town in the wilderness to a city. Finally, an influx of new settlers arrived in the mid-1880s with the completion of the railroads. David Denny, one of the original pioneers, felt the booming city needed a park and donated part of his original claim, which had been used as the city cemetery, for the city's first park (Denny Park). The graves were moved to the present site of Volunteer Park, at that time an unused 40-acre plot on Capitol Hill the city had purchased from James W. Colman. This became Washelli Cemetery. In the 1870s the bodies were moved again to the new Lake View Cemetery on its north side and the area became a park named City Park. The city almost sold the park in the early 1890s, but with the Klondike Gold Rush and the "City Beautiful" movement at the turn of the century, decided to develop the property and renamed it Volunteer Park to honor the U.S. volunteers in the Spanish American War.

The Olmsted Brothers firm designed the park to complement the swank "Millionaires'

Row" neighborhood on its south side and considered it the jewel of their park and boulevard plan for Seattle. The hill and park provided the perfect location for a gravity water system and reservoir to serve the growing city, which the city incorporated as part of the park.

In 1932 Dr. Richard Fuller and his mother donated money to build the Seattle Art Museum on the park grounds to house his priceless collection of Asian art. After a century, Volunteer Park today still is very much the elegant park the Olmsteds designed, taking advantage of its spectacular setting with gracious walkways, mature plantings and grand vistas.

The Walk

Start at the Fifteenth Avenue entrance of Volunteer Park at Galer. Follow the road as it begins a gradual climb to the hilltop. An imaginative children's playground with wading pool is on the right as you enter. If you go in summer you can see the spectacular dahlia garden on the left side of the road. A canine companion on leash would enjoy this walk.

Continue to the circle at the top of the hill. In front of the conservatory stands a larger-than-life statue of Secretary of State William Henry Seward who persuaded Congress to purchase Alaska, derisively called "Seward's Folly" at the time. Later his foresight was recognized. The purchase had a lasting impact on the citizens of Seattle who benefitted from the gold rush in the 1890s. This statue first stood on the grounds of the 1909 Alaska–Yukon–Pacific Exposition and has been here, temporarily, ever since.

Behind Seward, on the north side, stands an ornate Victorian Conservatory (1), reminiscent of London's "Crystal Palace," housing tropical and desert plants. Inside, enormous old palm trees, exotic orchids and ferns thrive in a moist tropical climate, along with begonias, cyclamen, angels' trumpets, hibiscus, New Zealand tree fern, and fiddle leaf figs. In other drier rooms there are collections of bromeliads and cacti. On a cold wet day this place can transport you to regions of warmth and beauty.

Originally, the road continued through to the cemetery where the conservatory now stands, and long funeral processions would wind their way through the posh neighborhood and park. After several alterations, the cemetery entrance was changed to its present location on Fifteenth Avenue.

From the conservatory, follow the path downhill to the west along the curving boulevard, past lawns, rhododendrons, mature trees and tennis courts. Pass a brick bandstand, popular in summer for outdoor concerts and at Easter for sunrise services. Bandstands were a standard feature of parks everywhere when the Olmsteds drew the designs; this current brick stage replaces earlier bandstands that succumbed to the elements.

You may stay on the road as it curves around all the way to the south side. Or, for a quieter walk, follow the path leading up to the reservoir built in 1901. From the rim of the reservoir look west to the shimmering city and Puget Sound, then back to the Seattle Asian Art Museum and through the Brazilian granite *Black Sun* sculpture (2) by Isamo Noguchi. Bring a camera at sunset to record the classic view here.

Continue on the road to the right around the reservoir to the 75-foot brick Gothic water tower (3) at the park's south border by East Prospect Street. Built in 1906, the water tower was called a standpipe and delivered 883,000 gallons of water at high pressure to a city that

relied on gravity for water pressure. The 108 steps to the top lead to one of the most magnificent views in the city, with an expansive view of the eastern horizon. There are also several panels that describe the tower's construction and tell about the Olmsted influence on Seattle's park system. Other panels help identify what you see.

Below the water tower, a path through the trees leads to a pool and, to its side, the Burke Monument, honoring Judge Thomas Burke who shaped Seattle's development for many years. He came to town as a poor attorney in 1878, and became a leader in all the important issues of the time: railroads, the Alaska-Yukon-Pacific Exposition, trade with Asia, and human rights.

At this point you may wish to continue south along Fourteenth Avenue, dubbed "Millionaires' Row," to see the fine turn-of-the century mansions that flanked the park and inspired the Olmsteds' grand design.

Or, stay in the park and continue north to the elegant Art Deco Asian Art Museum (4), designed by Carl Gould. Art collector Dr. Richard Fuller and his mother donated money for the museum in 1932 to house their Oriental jade and art collection, a real milestone in Seattle's cultural history. Exhibits inside change from time to time, but the two Ming Dynasty camels guarding the doorway have a timeless popularity. Generations of children have climbed up on them to "ride" the camels' backs. These are replicas of the marble originals, which are warm and dry in the downtown Seattle Art Museum. You may wish to visit the museum (closed Mondays) before resuming your walk.

Retrace your steps back down the hill through horse chestnuts, maples, hollies, spruce, redwood, Port Orford cedar, and pines. There's ample room on the grass for a picnic or a game of Frisbee on a good afternoon.

NOTES

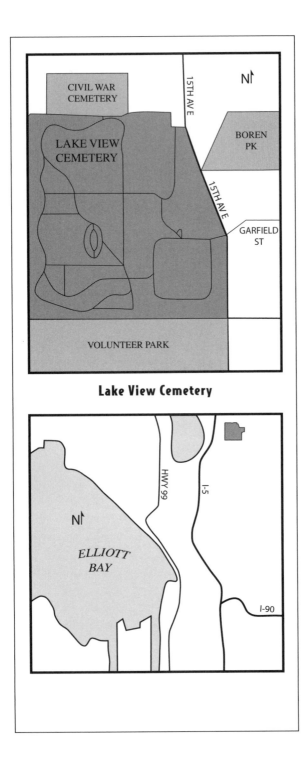

Lake View Cemetery

LAKE VIEW CEMETERY

Distance	2 miles
Time	1½ – 2 hours
Terrain	Moderate
Restrooms	No
Food	No

*S*eattle's early citizens were laid to rest on the high ridge overlooking their creation. With Lake View's stately old trees and intriguing headstones, you may wish to spend some time exploring this lovely Victorian cemetery.

Getting There

By Car: From I-5 heading north, take the Lakeview Boulevard exit (#168B). Turn left at the stop sign and head north. Continue straight, up the hill, as the road becomes Harvard. Turn right onto Boston and go up the hill to the traffic light. Stay on Boston as it curves around and becomes Fifteenth Avenue. Park your car near the Fifteenth Avenue East and East Garfield entrance to the cemetery. Or you may park in the cemetery.

From I-5 heading south, take the Roanoke exit (#168A), turn left across the freeway and turn right onto Tenth Avenue. At the traffic light at Boston, turn left and follow Boston as it curves around and becomes Fifteenth Avenue.

Metro: Take a #10 bus to the stop on Fifteenth Avenue East and East Galer.

Background

Seattle's early cemeteries followed the community's growth, with graves being moved to new "final resting places" as a matter of convenience. In the 1860s David Denny donated part of his claim for a city cemetery, which later became Denny Park, the city's first park. When the park was developed, the graves were moved to the site of the future Volunteer Park (see page 109), which at that time was an unused 40-acre plot on Capitol Hill. This became Washelli Cemetery, now in North Seattle. In 1873 the bodies were moved again, into Lake View Cemetery on the north side of the park.

The Walk

We recommend starting at Lake View Cemetery with the pioneers' graves, then going on to Volunteer Park to its south, but the walks may be done separately or combined with either Capitol Hill walk.

Note: There are no public restrooms in the cemetery, but there are some in Volunteer Park.

Start at the entrance to Lake View Cemetery at Fifteenth and Garfield. The cemetery has headstones representing many ethnic groups, familiar names of prominent citizens, and most of the city's first pioneers. The original view to the west is now blocked by large trees, but the view to the east is one of the city's best – Portage Bay, University of

Washington buildings, Lake Washington, and, on a clear day, the Cascades. Many of the trees are fine mature specimens from the turn of the century.

Walk west to the giant sequoia tree (1) on the highest knoll where headstones mark graves from the late 1800s and Seattle's founding fathers. The worn Carrara marble stone under the sequoia sits on Dr. David (Doc) Maynard's grave. Known as the most generous of Seattle's pioneers, he also was a heavy drinker and frequently in debt, which may explain Catherine Maynard's headstone: "She did what she could." Or perhaps it refers to the assistance she gave him as a nurse in Seattle's first hospital. After Doc's death she opened the city's first public reading room in her own home.

Walk north along the crown of the hill and cross the road on the right. The most visited graves in the cemetery are those of Bruce Lee and his son Brandon, located just east of the high ridge (2). Martial arts lovers come from long distances to pay their respects to them, and their graves are frequently adorned with remembrances. Continue north along the curve of the road and you will come to the elaborate pink granite gravestones for the Denny and Boren families, a reminder of the prominence they attained after founding our city. If you have time to explore further, walk to the south to see the grave for Princess Angeline, daughter of Chief Sealth, near those of Henry Yesler and his first wife. The grave site of Yesler's young second wife, Minnie Gagle Yesler, is empty, as she left the area soon after Henry died. Many pioneers' graves are located in the western part of the cemetery. For a thorough walking tour of their graves see Robert L. Ferguson's book, *The Pioneers of Lake View*.

Head north, then turn right and work your way east, back to the entrance. On the middle road there is a new granite mausoleum near the road. Farther east, a tall memorial shaft (3) memorializes American veterans of Japanese descent who died in World War II. Though their relatives had been incarcerated in internment camps, these Nisei volunteered for the toughest duty and had the highest decoration record of all U.S. regiments.

Looking through the fence on the north side of Lake View, you can see the small Civil War Cemetery across the street (4). It has graves of 200 local veterans of the Grand Army of the Republic. Until recently this unassuming cemetery was sadly neglected, but now local citizens, along with the City Parks Department, help maintain it. It is another of Seattle's historic sites. Unfortunately, there is no gate along the fence, so to reach it you have to go outside Lake View's front entrance and walk around.

As you leave Lake View, cross Fifteenth Avenue and walk north one block to East Olin Place. A dramatic steel sculpture stands in Louisa Boren Viewpoint (5). Named for the "Sweet Briar Bride" who was one of the city's original pioneers, this small park offers spectacular views of Lake Washington and the Cascades. Although David and Louisa were part of Seattle's founding families, they lost all their money in the 1893 Depression and were ostracized by the family, so are not buried in the family complex in Lake View. Perhaps this park gives Louisa some retribution. The massive English oaks along the bluff originally grew on Denny Hill before its regrade. Just beyond the most eastern oak a path begins that goes down through the park to Interlaken Boulevard below. (See page 131.)

To go on to Volunteer Park, retrace your steps along Fifteenth Avenue to the south, to the blinking red light at Galer and cross the street to the entrance of Volunteer Park.

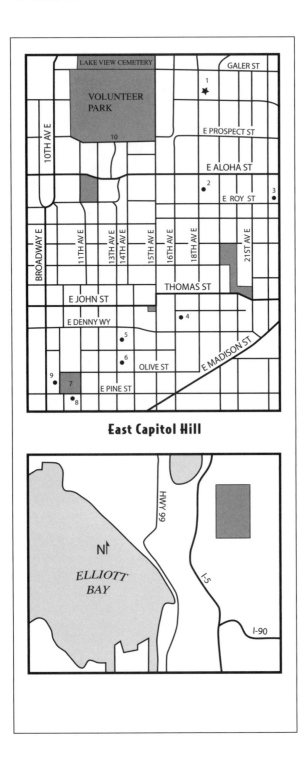

East Capitol Hill

EAST CAPITOL HILL

Distance	2½ miles round trip
Time	2 – 3 hours
Terrain	Mostly level, with an uphill grade at the end
Restrooms	In some public buildings
Food	Restaurants on Broadway

With Seattle's growth in the early 1900s and the expansion of streetcar lines, prosperous middle class families moved to new developments. The neighborhoods of East and South Capitol Hill feature large homes in a variety of turn-of-the century styles with nearby schools and churches to serve the neighborhood's families who lived nearby.

Getting There

By Car: From I-5 heading south, take the Roanoke exit #168A, turn left over the freeway, and turn right onto Tenth Avenue. At the traffic light at Boston, turn left and follow Boston as it curves around and becomes Fifteenth Avenue. Continue to the traffic light at Prospect. Park along the streets or in Volunteer Park.

From I-5 heading north, take the Lakeview Boulevard exit #168A. Turn left at the stop sign and head north. Continue straight, up the hill, as the road becomes Harvard. Turn right on Boston, up the hill. Stay on Boston as it curves around and becomes Fifteenth Avenue. Continue to the traffic light at Prospect. Park along the streets or in Volunteer Park.

Metro: Bus #10 from downtown stops along Fifteenth Avenue at both Galer and Prospect

Background

While the Harvard-Belmont area and Millionaires' Row became areas for turn-of-the century wealthy families, more modest middle class neighborhoods developed east of Volunteer Park, centered around churches and schools.

Sixteenth Avenue is a particularly pleasant street with many homes built from pattern book designs in a "Capitol Hill box" layout: The typical front porch has an entrance in the center, the living room on the right, the dining room on the left with the kitchen behind it. Upstairs there are four bedrooms in the corners. Garages are hidden on back alleys. Like all of Seattle, this area was logged before it was developed, and now the original turn-of-the century landscaping towers over the homes. Look for large monkey puzzle trees, which were popular at the time, and mature cedars and firs.

When families moved to the suburbs in the 1960s-1980s many of these large old houses were divided into apartments or neglected. With recent improvements in Seattle's schools and new affluence in Puget Sound, this neighborhood is once again alive with young families who are restoring the wooden homes' original colors and design features.

The Walk

This walk passes through a gracious turn-of-the-century neighborhood and the bustling street scene of Broadway. We start in the Stevens Neighborhood, east of Volunteer Park, named for the large elementary school on Galer and Eighteenth Avenue.

Start at Prospect and Fifteenth Avenue and walk east on Prospect to Sixteenth Avenue. Turn right onto Sixteenth and continue south.

Note: If you are continuing from the West Capitol Hill Walk, start at the Parker mansion, on Prospect and Fourteenth Avenue, just outside Volunteer Park, and walk east on Prospect to Sixteenth Avenue.

OPTION: *(Approximately one mile, through the neighborhood. This adds a couple of hills and about fifteen blocks to the walk.)*

At Sixteenth Avenue, turn left and walk north to Galer. Turn right onto Galer and walk two blocks to Eighteenth Avenue East to see the Stevens school (1), a classic turn-of-the-century school building that has recently been restored, at Eighteenth Avenue East and Galer. Turn right and head south on Eighteenth Avenue to see two of the area's largest Catholic institutions. St. Joseph's Catholic Church (2), Seattle's only Jesuit parish, is on the corner of Eighteenth Avenue and Aloha. Constrained by the Depression, the founders could not afford to build a traditional Gothic building and compromised with this early Art Deco style in reinforced concrete designed by Albertson, Wilson and Richardson. The result is a startlingly innovative church building and a Seattle Historic Landmark.

Turn left on Aloha and walk three blocks to the east. At Aloha and Twenty-first Avenue East is the massive Holy Names Academy (3). In the 1880s the Sisters of the Holy Names of Jesus and Mary came to

Seattle to establish a Catholic academy for high school girls. They brought a piano with them to teach the arts, and gradually expanded the school to include a kindergarten through eighth grade program as well. The Jackson regrade project forced them to abandon their first building. When the Sisters moved the academy from Beacon Hill in 1908 they were able to build this grand domed Renaissance-styled school. Generations of Seattle's Catholic girls have attended Holy Names.

Turn right onto Roy Street and return to Sixteenth Avenue.

Turn onto Sixteenth Avenue East and walk south on Sixteenth for several blocks. Near the back side of the Group Health hospital complex there are two old churches listed on the Seattle Historic Landmark register. The first, the former First Methodist Church on the corner of John Street, is a fine 1907 sandstone Gothic Revival building with period stained glass windows. No longer used as a church, it now serves as an architectural firm's office.

Before walking south to the second church, gaze at some of the Anhalt buildings across the street, currently part of the Group Health complex (4). Norman-styled former apartment buildings in dark clinker brick with leaded, stained glass windows enclose a small courtyard. There's time for a quick slide on the playground before continuing one block south to the First Church of Christ Scientist at East Denny Way. If the door of this Classic Revival sandstone building is open, walk inside to see its beautiful interior.

Turn right onto Denny. Walk past the church and go to Thirteenth Avenue East. Turn left onto Thirteenth Avenue East and walk south to the white Greek Orthodox Church of the Assumption (5), built in 1961. Every June it celebrates a Greek festival with

food, dancing, music, and tours of its sanctuary.

Continue walking south on Thirteenth Avenue.

In the middle of the next block find the stunning Russian Orthodox cathedral of St. Nicholas (6), named for the original fourth century St. Nicholas and as a memorial for the assassinated czar, Nicholas II. The diminuative yellow brick church has blue onion domes at each corner, icons over the door, Eastern crosses, and a larger central gold dome. Built in the small square plan of sixteenth century Russian cathedrals, it has a slender bell tower alongside it. Inside the sanctuary many Russian saints, including St. Nicholas, gaze down from the walls at worshipers.

Walk to the corner of Olive and turn right (west) past the brightly colored Morningside Academy, an alternative special needs school, to Lincoln Park and the Bobbie Morris Playfield (7), another Olmsted design. The Broadway Reservoir at Eleventh Avenue East and East Pine was dedicated as a public park in 1901 and still helps to supply the community's water. Today its fountain and surrounding park offer a bit of peace and green space close to the mass of shops and crowds on Broadway.

Across Pine Street, the newly restored Odd Fellows Hall (8) is a turn-of-the-century jewel. Built in 1908, the ornate sandstone brick building with terra cotta trim was a haven for early Seattleites. Gaze upward to the pediment and decorative dentils. Just below, its gleaming gold and green shield contains three rings standing for friendship, love and truth. The ground floor now has retail outlets, but the second floor contains four performance spaces, popular with music, film and theater groups, and the large Century Ballroom. Disney restored the ballroom in the mid-1990s as a set for a movie senior prom. Today it is used for dance classes and public dances.

Walk west on Pine to Broadway, the heart of Capitol Hill, and turn right (north) onto Broadway.

At one time this was the road from downtown for funeral processions to Lake View

Cemetery. It has also been called the city's oldest suburban shopping district and the city's first auto row. Henry Ford came to Broadway in 1909 to greet the winners of the New York to Seattle Auto Race. Nowadays it is a gathering place for people with diverse lifestyles.

On the west side is the massive Broadway Performance Hall (9), originally Broadway High School, surrounded by newer Seattle Central Community College buildings. Jimi Hendrix is enshrined in a classic pose on the sidewalk on the east side. Farther along, the sidewalks are paved with inset dance steps. Take a quick dance on Jack Maki's inlaid bronze feet on the east side of Broadway. There are many restaurants and coffee shops along the way where you can fortify yourself before returning to your car. A Seattle classic is Dick's Drive In; more upscale is Septième, and there are several ethnic restaurants and cafes.

Take any cross street off Broadway and head uphill to Fourteenth Avenue. Walk north along Fourteenth Avenue, the original Millionaires' Row, to see more of this neighborhood as you return to your car or bus. The south entrance to Volunteer Park is at Fourteenth Avenue and Prospect (10). See page 109 for Volunteer Park walk.

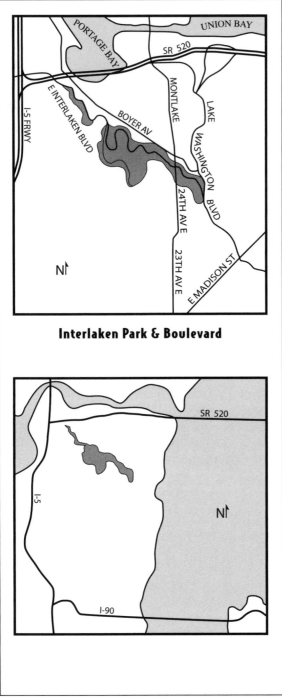

Interlaken Park & Boulevard

INTERLAKEN PARK AND BOULEVARD

Distance	3 miles
Time	1-2 hours
Terrain	Fairly level, except for woodland trails
Restrooms	No
Food	No

Perhaps no Seattle park illustrates Olmsted's vision more clearly than this winding boulevard along the edge of a ravine, where once an evergreen forest stood. Steep paths branching off from the gracious roadway offer contrasting walks through this park.

Getting There

By Car: From I-5 heading north, take the Lakeview exit, #168A, and bear left at the stop sign. Where the road forks, go straight, up the hill, and continue as it curves and becomes Miller Street. Turn left at the traffic light onto Tenth Avenue. Head north on Tenth Avenue, and turn right at the traffic light onto Roanoke and right again at the second street onto Interlaken Boulevard. This is just after Miller Street, below the Seattle Prep campus. A small rock pillar on the left side of the road marks the beginning of Interlaken Boulevard. Park along the road after the park entrance.

From I-5 heading south: Take the East Roanoke freeway exit, #168A, turn left onto Roanoke and drive east across the freeway. Stay in the left-hand lane at the intersection of Tenth Avenue East. Turn right at the second street onto Interlaken Boulevard, as above.

Metro: Bus #25 goes to Boyer and Fuhrman Avenue on the west; bus #12 goes to Galer and Nineteenth Avenue, the middle of the walk.

Background

*"Landscape moves us in a manner more nearly
analogous to music than to anything else.
Gradually and silently the charm overcomes us;
we know not exactly where or how."*

—Frederick Law Olmsted

At the turn of the last century Seattleites became mad for bicycles and sought new bike paths. Most city streets at that time were paved with planks, which were difficult to ride on. The city engineer George Cotterill, an ardent bicycle fan, found routes for bike trails between Volunteer Park and Washington Park. His cinder-surfaced paths became Interlaken Boulevard and the beginning of Seattle's present extensive boulevard system. The Olmsteds approved this Interlaken stretch as a link between downtown to the Boulevard System. At that time Interlaken's spectacular views of mountains and lakes made it very popular.

The lush old evergreen forest that filled the hillside was completely logged off by the turn of the century and present mature maples and alders have gradually grown in its place. The park's steep slopes and extensive logging have aggravated problems with stability, creating landslides and deep gullies in some places. The Seattle Parks Department and Friends of Interlaken Park are working to replant the area with native plants to restabilize the area.

The Walk

Caution: There are no sidewalks on the first portion of the walk, but you will find few cars on the road, and those will be going slowly as they negotiate the many curves. This is a good walk for a canine companion on a leash.

The magical quality of Interlaken begins immediately as you enter the Boulevard and wend your way through enormous ancient maples and alders. Below to the east and north are window vistas onto Portage Bay, the University of Washington campus, eastside suburbs and the Cascades. But the road keeps turning and beckoning you onward. A few unobtrusive private homes and driveways occur, but nothing interferes with the glorious woodland feel of the road. Banks on the high side of the road are clothed in sword ferns. If you can choose a season, walk this one in the fall, when color brightens the trees, and as the leaves fall, views begin to widen.

About a half mile from the entry pillar you will encounter a rock along the right side of the road with a plaque. The five acres uphill to your right were dedicated in 1913 as Boren Park in honor of Louisa Boren, the "Sweet Briar Bride." A steep winding trail leads to a spectacular lookout at Boren Point above. (See the Lake View Cemetery walk, page 117.)

A little farther along on Interlaken the boulevard branches. Take the right fork, onto Interlaken Drive East. In about a half mile you will come to a historic structure on your right, the Seattle Hebrew Academy, formerly Forest

Ridge Convent and School. Just past the
school's driveway you emerge from the woods
at the intersection with East Galer. Across the
street to the right is the historic Stevens
School, recently restored for neighborhood
children. On the left there is a notice board
that describes community work on the park, a
map and a bird list.

Keeping the park on your left, turn left
onto East Galer and bear left downhill onto
Crescent. Turn left again on Twentieth Avenue
East and follow the road down as it curves and
becomes Twenty-first Avenue East, and continues down to Interlaken Place. You'll find a
paved trail opening at the bottom with another
notice board and map. This is East Interlaken
Boulevard, which is open only to walkers and
bike riders. You step immediately from a city

street back under the umbrella of a northwest forest, this time with more evergreens to enjoy. Follow this road northwest where it reconnects with the original Interlaken Boulevard. There are several dirt paths along this stretch that may beckon you, depending on your time and interest.

Continue north along the boulevard to your car or bus.

You should arrive feeling refreshed and thankful for the vision of those who preserved this pocket of enduring beautiful Northwest forest inside the city for us to enjoy.

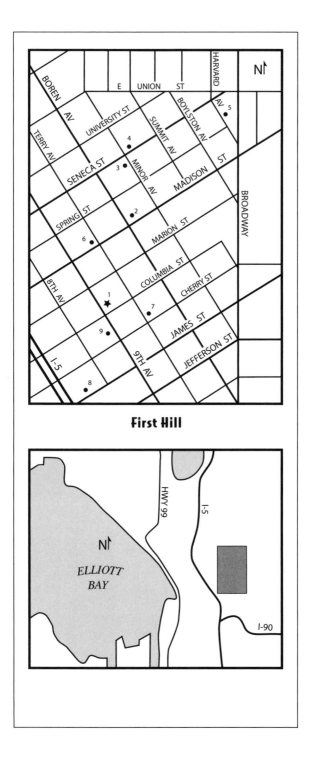

First Hill

FIRST HILL

Distance	1½ miles
Time	2 – 2½ hours
Terrain	Moderate (except for one hill)
Restrooms	In public buildings
Food	Restaurants along the way

A mong Seattle's many hills, First Hill was where Seattle's prominent first families settled at the turn of the century with their new wealth. Now much changed both physically and socially, it offers a glimpse of Seattle history.

Getting There

By Car: From I-5 take the James Street exit. Head east (uphill) of the freeway. Turn left onto either Eighth or Ninth avenues and park on the street or in hospital parking lots.

Metro: Bus #3 or #4 bus goes to Ninth and James; #12 goes to Eighth and Madison.

Background

As daunting as Seattle's hills are today, they are mere nubs compared to the original hills faced by the pioneers. Nearly 100 regrades have changed the city's topography, leveling some of the steepest peaks like Denny Hill, and filling in deep ravines and tideflats.

A 344-foot hill above the original center of Seattle was named "Profanity Hill" by those who had to climb it. Both the loggers who climbed it to cut trees, and later lawyers who trekked up it to reach the county court house, became breathless and profane about its steepness. Streams and springs ran down its slopes into the bay. Boarding and rooming houses sprang up where trees had been logged and the land cleared. When streetcars made First Hill accessible, the first families built their large homes, social clubs and churches in the area.

Over the years most of the area's grand houses have been taken down. Today the dominant buildings are clinics and hospitals, giving rise to its newer nickname, "Pill Hill." This walk also features three of Seattle's most distinctive and historic churches.

The Walk

Start at Ninth Avenue, north of Cherry, and walk north along Ninth to St. James Cathedral (1). Designed by the architects who designed St. John the Divine in New York, this distinctive landmark with its 150-foot twin spires was completed in 1907. When built, the spires were separated by a large central dome which collapsed under a huge snowfall in 1916. Luckily the cathedral was empty at the time. The Italian Renaissance building is built of light tan brick with stained glass windows, limestone statues, and delicate carved paneling. Its mammoth pipe organ is played for special

concerts as well as regular services. In a 1996 remodel after a disastrous fire the altar of this Seattle Historic Landmark was moved to the center of the cathedral.

Exit through the side door and walk up to Terry Avenue. Turn left onto Terry and walk past the empty lot. That is all that is left of the 1915 Cabrini Hospital named in honor of St. Francis Cabrini – a large hole. The Perry Retirement Community is planned for the site. Turn right onto Madison and walk one block east to Boren Street.

At Boren, go kitty corner across the street to reach the University Club (2) on the northeast corner of Madison. Built by Martin van Buren Stacy in 1889, this was originally a private home typical of the mansions of early First Hill. The Queen Anne-styled building with decorative trim is the oldest of the remaining four mansions on First Hill, and has belonged to the University Club since 1901.

Continue north on Boren one block to Spring Street. The 1902 residence on the corner with Roman brick and Moorish terra cotta arches, known as W. D. Hofius house, served for more than 50 years as the home of Seattle's Catholic bishops.

Walk one block east on Spring to the corner of Minor, turn left onto Minor to see another interesting old First Hill home. The Dearborn House (3), at 1117 Minor Avenue (the corner of Seneca), built in 1909, is now the headquarters of Historic Seattle, which is restoring it. It may be open for an informal tour. Both it and the Hofius house are examples of First Hill's elegant turn-of-the-century mansions.

One of the grandest mansions of them all is kitty-corner across Seneca at 1204 Minor Avenue. The Stimson-Green Mansion (4) is listed on both the Seattle and National Registers of Historic Places. Designed by Kirtland Cutter, this half-timbered English Arts and Crafts mansion was built in 1901 for C. D. Stimson who started the Stimson mill in Ballard in 1889, the year of the Great Seattle Fire. It was the girlhood home of Seattle television entrepreneur Dorothy Stimson Bullitt. From 1914-1975 it was owned by Joshua Green, a wealthy banker who lived in the house until his death at 105. Slated for demolition after his death, it was rescued by Historic Seattle and The Preservation Authority. With seventeen rooms and six fireplaces, its elegant furnishings still look much as they did in 1901. Today the mansion is one of a few reminders of the elegant life on First Hill, where ladies called on one another in horse-drawn carriages and held formal parties under gas chandeliers. Present owner, Patsy Bullitt Collins, granddaughter of Stimson, runs a catering business here, hosting weddings, parties and receptions. Call 206-624-0474 to arrange a tour.

Next to it on Minor at University Street is the First Hill Park, where at one time Stimson horses were stabled.

Turn right onto University Street and walk one block to Summit. Turn left onto Summit.

At East Union and Summit see the former Summit Grade School. This 1905 wooden building is also on the Seattle Landmarks Register. For a time it was the campus of Seattle Community College, and is now a the Northwest School for the Performing Arts, a private high school.

Continue heading east on University Street and head east for a few blocks. At the corner of Harvard stands the solid 1913 Knights of Columbus Building. Across the street at 1400 Harvard Avenue is the rehabilitated Fire Station #25. One of Seattle's earliest firehouses, it was surplused in 1970, and bought by Historic Seattle. Sold again, it was remodeled into townhouses. It retains its original tile roof and old arched windows.

Turn right onto Harvard Avenue to reach our second church, the beautiful First Baptist Church at 1121 Harvard Avenue (5). Built in Gothic Revival style, its copper-clad 160-foot tower and spire rise high above this 1912 Seattle Historic Landmark. Public events, such as oratorios, lectures and poetry readings, are often held in its spacious sanctuary.

Go back south along Harvard to busy Madison Street to find coffee houses, ethnic restaurants and fast food places from which to fortify yourself before going on. At this point you may wish to cross Broadway to visit the Seattle University campus to the southeast.

If not, turn right onto Madison. Walk a couple of blocks west on Madison. In the middle of the block between Summit and Minor on the right side, in front of the banks' parking lots you will pass the historic street clock at 1200 Madison, a favorite meeting point for early First Hill residents.

Across Madison are several buildings of the Swedish Medical Center complex. On the south corner of Madison and Boren is a new wing of the Center, on the site of pioneer Morgan Carkeek's mansion. The home was demolished in 1939, but in this wing you can find a lobby display telling the history of First Hill and of Swedish Medical Center. Dr. Nils Johanson built a small hospital near here in 1910 with contributions from ten Swedish-American friends. Two years later they acquired a larger hospital located nearby at Summit and Columbia when its founder, Dr. Rininger, was killed just before it was to open. They named it Swedish Hospital instead of Summit as Rininger had planned so all the linens monogrammed with the letters "S.H." were still usable.

Other "Pill Hill" hospitals are Virginia Mason Medical Center at Ninth and Seneca, named by Dr. James Tate Mason and his partner Dr. John Blackford for Mason's daughter Virginia. Harborview Hospital is on the hilltop at Ninth Avenue and Jefferson, nearby in the Central District, on the site of the hill's first court house which made the huffing, puffing lawyers so angry. Harborview Hospital is owned by King County and managed by the University of Washington as a teaching hospital.

Continue west down Madison to Terry to reach the Sorrento Hotel (6) on the corner. The elegant Mediterranean-styled building was called the "Honeymoon Hotel" when it opened in 1908. To capitalize on Seattle's harbor view, the architect put the dining room on the top floor – now it's tucked in on the first floor. Look for a fountain in its diamond-shaped courtyard, rimmed with palm trees. If you would like a special treat, walk in and order tea in the hotel's mahogany-paneled lobby by a cozy fire. You will feel you have traveled to another part of the world.

When you are rested, walk south along Terry, past O'Dea High School, a 1923 Tudor-styled boys' school in the Catholic Archdiocese.

Continue south on Terry to the corner of Cherry for a visit to the Frye Art Museum (7). Charles and Emma Frye were a prominent Seattle couple at the turn of the century. He made his fortune as a meat packer, and gave his collection of European nineteenth century paintings and the museum to the city, with the condition that admission be free. In 1997 the museum was remodeled and expanded. Notice that many of the paintings he collected are of animals – as might appeal to a meat packer. The museum's restaurant is open from 11-4.

Walk to the corner of James Street and head down James to Eighth Avenue to the Trinity Episcopal Church (8), the last of our churches. A traditional English Country Gothic-style stone building with a spire, Trinity is Seattle's oldest church in continuous use and is listed on the National Register of Historic Places. The original Trinity chapel at Third Avenue and Jefferson was destroyed in the Great Seattle Fire of 1889. The congregation moved up the hill and built another church at Eighth Avenue and James, but in 1902 it too burned down. The current building was built the following year on the same site and has German stained glass windows and the organ that came "around the Horn" for the second church and survived the fire. Catch your breath in its charming courtyard. Today the congregation reaches out to the urban community with a Northwest Harvest food bank, a thrift store, and inner city church services.

Climb back up the hill to Ninth Avenue. Turn left on Ninth, walk a block and cross Cherry. In the middle of the next block the German Club at 613 Ninth Avenue (9) was built as the federal assay office following the Klondike Gold Rush to measure and store millions of dollars in gold. It had its own melting department to make gold bars from the miners' gold dust. Since 1935 the building has been the social center for the German Club.

Return to your car or bus.

NOTES

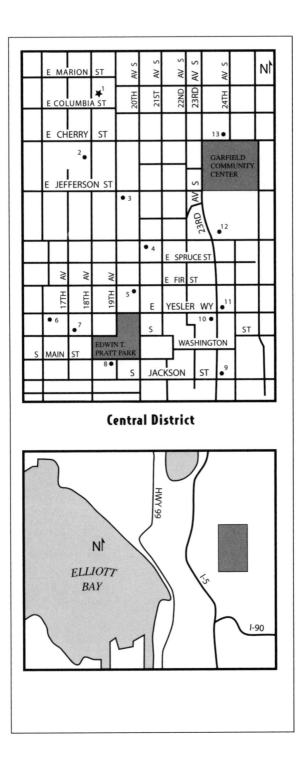

Central District

CENTRAL DISTRICT

Distance	2 miles
Time	2 hours
Terrain	Moderate with some hills
Restrooms	In parks and some public buildings
Food	In restaurants and shops

*A*s succeeding waves of working class people settled in the Northwest they typically formed their own communities in the Central Area — it was first a Jewish enclave, then black, and currently the Asian community is expanding. From impressive public buildings to rundown and resurrected neighborhoods, the history of the Central District is the history of Seattle.

Getting There

By Car: Take I-5 to exit #166, Madison Street heading north, or Marion Street heading south. Drive to East Madison and turn east onto Madison. Continue on Madison until Eighteenth Avenue. Turn right (south) on Eighteenth Avenue and go to Marion Street. The Immaculate Conception Church is at the corner of Eighteenth Avenue and Marion Street. Or, you can drive along Twenty-third

Avenue to Marion and turn west to Eighteenth Avenue. Limited parking is available behind the church and on nearby neighborhood streets.

Metro: Buses #2 and #8 along Twenty-third Avenue East.

Background

One of Seattle's most eclectic areas, the Central District lies above the International District and First Hill, between Madison Street and I-90. Many homes, churches and public agencies remain only partly touched by time, surviving through several owners and users, while others have been altered by political and social upheavals.

Soon after Seattle's first pioneers arrived in 1851, Manuel Lopes, the area's first African American, opened a barbershop in Pioneer Square. In 1859 black pioneers William and Sarah Grose arrived, six years after he had sailed to Japan with Commander Perry. At Governor Stevens' invitation Grose became manager of the town's second hotel and restaurant, Our House, in 1876. In 1882 he bought Henry Yesler's 12-acre farm on the south side of Madison Street for $1,000 in gold coins. After his restaurant burned down in the Great Seattle Fire of 1889, Grose began to subdivide his land to sell to other African- Americans.

This area became the Central District. Two distinct black areas emerged: one a residential area in the hilly forested East Madison area, and the other, a working class, transient neighborhood consisting of lodging houses and saloons catering to sailors, loggers and railroad workers between Yesler and Jackson streets near the International District.

After the Great Seattle Fire destroyed many homes in the original part of the city in

1889, wealthy citizens moved to First Hill and Queen Anne Hill. The white middle class built homes in the Central District, which was served by a trolley up Yesler and down Twenty-third Avenue. By 1900 the East Madison area had the largest concentration of black homeowners in the city, but the total black population in both districts was only 400. Fifteen years later 2,500 new black Seattleites 1940s the demand for workers in shipyards and the aircraft industry caused the great black migration of 15,000, portrayed in the paintings of Jacob Lawrence. The neighborhood deteriorated during the urban renewal and social upheaval of the 1960s and suburban flight lasted until recently, when families started to return to the old homes that had been left behind.

Today there is a renewed interest in the Central District because of its proximity to downtown, affordable land, and stunning views. Homes are being repaired and renovated, with much of their Victorian charm restored. Look for gingerbread on rooflines, multiple gables, fishscale shingles, bumped out bay windows, cupolas, turrets, and balcony railings with intricate fretwork. Many of these details have been ripped off and the exteriors simplified or neglected, while other homes are being meticulously restored. On some streets entire houses are so similar to their neighbors you can tell they were ordered from catalogs popular at the turn of the century.

The Central Area Development Association (CADA) is working on a community promenade that will link Garfield High School and Washington Middle School, and planting trees throughout the district. Senior volunteers and the disabled are helping to upgrade local real estate.

In addition to the bakery and coffee shops on Twenty-third Avenue and Jackson, you may be tempted by barbecue on Yesler Way, up from the Langston Hughes Center, Ezell's Fried Chicken near the end of the walk, or several soul food restaurants along the way.

The Walk

Start your walk at the Immaculate Conception Church, on Eighteenth Avenue at Marion, a century-old church on the National Historic Register that reflects local social and economic history. Built in 1904 by immigrant Catholic craftsmen in six months time for $65,000, this handsome church replaced an earlier church on this site. Despite a devastating fire, in 1991 the congregation celebrated their centennial and the building has just been restored. Its newly painted twin domes once again gleam in the afternoon sun. Immaculate Conception's architectural style is a mixture. It has neo-Baroque wooden steeples and cupolas, Romanesque arches and a Gothic layout.

Many Catholic minorities moved to this area during the Civil Rights movements of the 1960s, as exemplified by statues of St. Martin of Peru, St. Vincent of the Philippines, St. Teresa, St. Clare and St. Joseph in the church's sanctuary. The crucifix over the altar has a Black Christ.

Next door on Eighteenth Avenue the Seahawks Academy, a middle school operated as a public-private enterprise by the Seattle Schools and the Seattle Seahawks, was the original parish school. The colorful Immaculate P-Patch community garden flourishes on the corner of Columbia Street.

Continue walking south along Eighteenth Avenue. In the next block the old Fire Station No. 23 (1) houses the Central Area Motivation

Program – CAMP. Built in 1909, it boasts the huge red doors of the old firehouse, a wing that once served as the stable for the horses that pulled the engine, and an intricate brick patterned exterior – all capped with a tile roof. CAMP offers housing assistance, job training, and a food bank. The Firehouse Mini Park beside it has a play area with an imaginative model fire engine.

Continue walking south on Eighteenth Avenue a couple of blocks to Cherry Street. On the west side of the street are the original buildings of Providence Medical Center (2), now part of Swedish Medical Center. The oldest dates to 1910, with additional wings added in 1966, 1978, and 1990. Look for its central brick tower topped with a terra cotta pyramid and cross. Built by the Sisters of Providence to serve the Central District's mill operators and other blue collar workers, this hospital was the first in the nation to offer coupons for health care to the poor. The hospital's original designer, Mother Joseph, raised money by marketing a patent medicine and by "begging tours." Providence's parking garages and medical offices now extend several blocks beyond the first building but lack its classic Beaux Arts style.

From the hospital, continue to the corner of Jefferson; cross the street and turn left onto Jefferson and walk one block east to Nineteenth Avenue. Cross Nineteenth and admire the Camden Apartments (3) building on the corner. First built as a one-family home, it then became a convalescent home before its present use as apartments. Behind the ungainly addition in the front of the building is one of the district's best preserved Victorian structures with its gabled tower, dentil moldings, and fish scale shingle trim. Note the Victorian fan details at the corners of bays.

Continue walking one more block east on Jefferson to Twentieth Avenue. Turn right onto Twentieth and walk to Spruce Street. The large brick building on the corner is the former Odessa Brown Children's Clinic (4), built as the Herzl synagogue, which is now housed on Mercer Island. Many beautiful and valuable temples were left behind during the flight to the suburbs in the 1960s. Some of the Stars of David on cornerstones of this brick building have been removed and "Odessa Brown Children's Clinic" has been added to the concrete pediment. The Black Panthers started a children's facility here in 1963 and named the clinic after the woman who had worked so hard to obtain health care for the black community. This building now serves as the County Health Education offices.

Across the street on the west corner, the low People's Wall is all that remains of the Black Panther's 1960s headquarters, once located where homes are today. Painted by Dion Henderson and Panthers' supporters, its fading mural paintings include a portrait of Malcom X. The Panthers were a powerful community force during this time – very active in politics as well as tutoring children and delivering free breakfast to local residents.

Continue south on Twentieth Avenue one block to East Fir Street and cross East Fir. The Tolliver Temple (5) was once a synagogue of the Sephardic Jewish congregation Bikur Holim, which has since moved to the Seward Park neighborhood. Built in 1929, the building is in Romanesque Revival style with brick and Art-Deco concrete arches. Several Stars of David are still visible.

Walk west on Fir to Eighteenth Avenue, turn left (south) on Eighteenth Avenue and go to Yesler, a busy thoroughfare with small busi-

nesses, community services and restaurants. Cross Yesler and walk down to Seventeenth Avenue. The magnificent Langston Hughes Performing Arts Center (6) is in the middle of the block. This was formerly the synagogue of the Congregation Bikur Cholim, now in the Seward Park neighborhood. Designed by theater architect B. Marcus Priteca in 1912, it has a stunning Byzantine dome, and neo-classical pilasters in white brick with terra cotta trim. (Priteca is best known for the theaters he designed for Alexander Pantages, such as the Palomar and the Coliseum, now Banana Republic.) Walk around the building to see its classic details. The theater is one of the finest performing arts spaces in the city, with its dome centered over the stage. Some of its Jewish symbols have been covered over, including the Ten Commandments above the door, but you can visualize places where Stars of David used to be. The City bought the building in 1970 with money from the Model Cities Program. Now operated by the Seattle Parks and Recreation Department, it features dance, music, karate, and dramatic events. Because of its intimacy and fine acoustics, jazz musicians enjoy performing here.

Go to the south side of the Langston Hughes Center and turn left on South Washington Street. Walk to Eighteenth Avenue to the Edwin T. Pratt Park (7), named for Pratt, an influential president of the Urban League who was murdered in the doorway of his home in 1969. The Urban League started many self-help and equal rights programs, including the Central Area Motivation Program (CAMP) and the Seattle Opportunities Industrialization Center, all of which influenced the development of this area.

The park provides a covered play area, sport court, P-Patch, and children's park. The wading pool is shaped like a map of Africa, with examples of African art around its perimeter. In 1958 the city bought this land for Washington Middle School, but built the school one block east. Instead, in 1966 it built the park here near the Yesler Terrace Housing Project with Forward Thrust community improvement money.

At this point you have a choice: You may continue heading east through the park, past the children's play area to Twentieth Avenue. Walk down Washington Street, to the Dr. Blanche Lavisso Park, named after the first medical director of Odessa Brown. Walk through the park and follow the covered walk to the right to Jackson Street. The walkway and amphitheater are the beginning of an urban trail, Promenade 23, that will eventually go between Garfield High School and Washington Middle School, providing a central park trail to link the community. At the moment it is only a few blocks long. Or, go to the south end of the Edwin T. Pratt Park at the corner of Nineteenth Avenue and South Main to the Pratt Fine Arts School (8). Originally a one-man bakery, then a former Wonder Bread Bakery garage, the building has recently been remodeled into a teaching facility and studio. A hidden gem, the Pratt is nationally recognized for its classes in ceramics, forging, glassblowing, jewelry, painting, and sculpture. Continue to Jackson Street and peek through the windows on the Jackson Street side to watch the artists at work blowing glass or forging metal. If you would like to make a bakery stop at this point, there is a Gai's Variety Bread thrift outlet store with delicious choices across the street.

From either route turn left on Jackson and walk east.

Seattle Vocational Institute, the new building on South Jackson on the east side of Dr. Blanche Lavisso Park, offers job skill training to train local people for community jobs as one of Seattle Central Community College's programs.

Continue up Jackson to the corner of Twenty-third Avenue (9). Spurred by incentives from the Central Area Development Association and HUD money, this area is becoming the commercial hub of the Central District. The new Starbucks features photos of jazz greats Charlie Parker and Ben Webster and local jazz and rock musicians, such as Quincy Jones and Jimi Hendrix. A video store and drug store have also opened on this corner. National retail chains have created the anchor, encouraging banks to begin to lend to others.

Turn left (north) on Twenty-third Avenue. You can't miss Fire Station No. 6 at Twenty-third Avenue and East Yesler Way (10), built in 1931 in Art Deco style of cast concrete with red steel doors. The 1987 addition was built in the original style. Neon lightning bolts above the doors light up and pulsate when a fire alarm sounds.

Plans are afoot to rescue the three 1900-era Victorian wooden homes across the street – supposedly to make them into condominiums. Notice the charcoal writing all over the exterior of the corner house. They are very fragile and dilapidated today, but their style is unmistakable.

The Douglass-Truth Library (11) on the east side Twenty-third was originally called the Yesler Branch Library, but was renamed for Frederick Douglass and Sojourner Truth in a community contest in the 1960s. Unlike the Carnegie libraries of the period, this Italian Renaissance-style building was built with city funds. The library's collection reflects current community ethnicity: There were more Japanese and Yiddish holdings in the 1930s, but today it contains the largest collection of black literature in the Northwest.

Continue walking north along Twenty-third Avenue a few blocks to Alder Street and the James B. Garfield High School (12). Built in 1923 after old Broadway High had been outgrown, the original brick Jacobean building with terra cotta trim has had many additions. Classic details on the parapet above the north main door are a globe, harp, medical shield, and sheaf of grain. The class of 1945 donated the school's rhododendrons as a memorial for those lost in World War II. In 1962, 51 percent of the school's population was black. Optional city busing to other schools began the next year but ended in 1997. Today Garfield is a magnet school for science and music and boasts Seattle's highest number of National Merit Scholars. Garfield alumni we recognize are Kung Fu artist Bruce Lee, musicians Quincy Jones and Jimi Hendrix, Olympic Gold Medalist Debbie Armstrong, and civic leader Jack Benaroya.

Continue north along Twenty-third Avenue. The Garfield Community Center, Field House and Medgar Evers Swimming Pool were built with Forward Thrust funds and are the civic center of the community. Public restrooms are available here. You may walk one block east to see the Horace Mann School at Twenty-fourth and East Cherry (13). A Georgian Colonial Revival building built in 1901, it now is used for community programs. Or continue along Twenty-third Avenue and return to your car by way of Cherry (a fairly steep hill), Columbia or Marion.

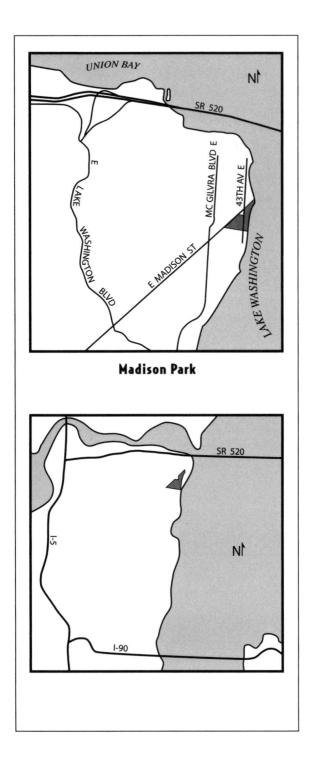

Madison Park

MADISON PARK

Distance	½ mile
Time	½ hour
Terrain	Level with broad walkways
Restrooms	In the waterfront park
Food	Nearby restaurants

Once the site of a colorful amusement park, Madison Park is now a quiet neighborhood park with a broad beach perfect for summer swimming and winter bonfires. At any time of year you can get great views of Lake Washington as you walk along the level shoreline.

Getting There

By Car: Head east on Madison to Forty-third East at the foot of East Madison and park along the street.

Metro: Bus #11 goes to Forty-third and McGilvra – the end of the line.

Background

Judge John J. McGilvra came to Seattle in 1861 from Chicago where he had practiced law with Abraham Lincoln. After Lincoln became president, he appointed McGilvra United States District Attorney for Washington Territory. Later McGilvra became a private attorney in Seattle and was involved with many of the city's major projects. In the 1860s he bought 420 acres in Madison Park from the University of Washington. He then built a road (the present Madison Street) from downtown to the shore of Lake Washington and subsidized the street's cable car, which went to McGilvra's Landing, the resort he built at the lake shore. First developed into an amusement park along the shoreline, the Madison Park Pavilion held a 500-seat pavilion, floating bandstand, boat house, racetrack, and a ball park, home to the Northwest League baseball champions. The Pavilion began by offering family entertainment, but later became a beer hall.

In 1890 McGilvra bought an additional twenty-one acres from the university for five dollars an acre and created Madison Park, which he used to attract customers to his Madison Street Cable Car Company. A little passenger boat provided cruises around the lake departing from the park's dock. McGilvra accommodated long-term summer residents by building platforms on which tents could be set up, possibly the city's first houseboats. The only buildings he allowed were cottages he rented on an annual basis.

After the turn of the twentieth century the city bought the park from the Seattle Electric Company and refurbished it for the 1909 Alaska-Yukon-Pacific Exposition. It was briefly called "White City Park." In 1914 the Port of

Seattle built the first double-ended car ferry, the *Leschi,* to carry traffic across Lake Washington between Madison Park and Kirkland. In the 1920s, long after cottage rental and the other enterprises were no longer profitable, the McGilvra estate sold the remaining lots to the city to be added to the park. Note: This is one of the few parks in the city that the Olmsteds did not design – apparently they did not think it offered much potential!

Today a swimming and picnic area along the lake shore make this a popular park from late spring through fall. The beach includes a bathhouse, raft with diving boards, and roped swimming areas for children.

Across Forty-third Avenue, Richard Beyer's granite animals known as *McGilvra's Farm* roam the community park and provide great climbing for kids.

A little farther south on Forty-third East, the Pioneer Hall at Madison Park (1642 Forty-third East), built in 1910, is a community center and museum containing historic photographs and documents. It is open from 1-4 P.M. on the second Sunday of every month.

The Walk

Start at the north side of the lakeshore park at the end of Madison Street and head south. Cross over Forty-third Avenue to check out the playground. After walking along the waterfront you may want to explore the residential area nearby or stop for a snack in the village.

Madison Park is about two miles north of Madrona Park through a lovely neighborhood. You may want to join the two walks together.

Going to Madrona: Head east on Madison Street a few blocks to McGilvra Boulevard and turn left onto McGilvra. Continue walking south on McGilvra. Bear left at Lake Washington

Boulevard onto it and left again at Madrona
Drive. Return along the same route.

NOTES

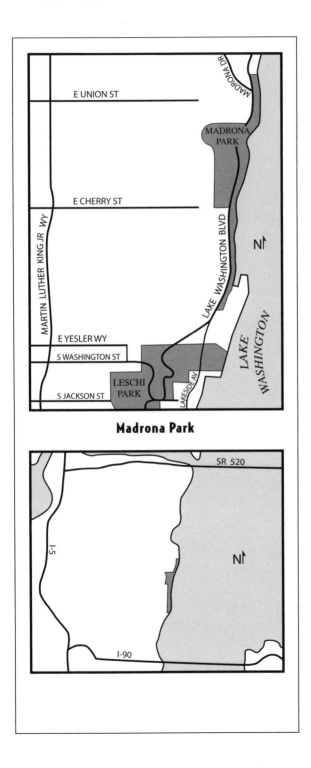

Madrona Park

MADRONA PARK

Distance	½ mile
Time	½ hour
Terrain	Level
Restrooms	In summer
Food	In summer

*T*he northern-most of the Olmsted parks along Lake Washington, Madrona Park was created in 1916 when the lake was lowered as part of the locks project. The newly exposed shoreline, with the exquisite views of Mount Rainier, fit perfectly with the "City Beautiful" movement of the time.

Getting There

By Car: From I-5, drive east on Yesler to the Leschi "bird." Take either road down to Lake Washington Boulevard and turn left. The park is on Lake Washington Boulevard, where Madrona Drive meets Lake Washington Boulevard.

Or, heading east on Madison, turn right on McGilvra, and head south to Lake Washington Boulevard and continue to the park. There is a parking lot on the south side of the park.

Metro: Bus #2 to Madrona Drive.

Background

Like Leschi Park to the south, Madrona Park originally had a hotel and boat launching facility to attract people to the new residential development nearby. It was first used as a private trolley park by the Seattle Electric Company, which operated a scenic trolley line from the top of the hill to the beach. In 1888 developers built a cable car from downtown to make the lots accessible to future home owners. It must have worked – ten years later the Madrona neighborhood had developed into a small community.

The Olmsted Brothers design linked Madrona, Leschi and Madison parks along the lake shore with greenbelts and broad boulevards, perfect for touring by bicycle or car. In recent years Bicycle Sunday and a 12-kilometer foot race have made use of the Madrona facilities.

Named for the native madrona trees that leaned out over the water, the park was developed beneath the old-growth forest with trails leading through it. In the early 1900s, when the level of the lake was lowered nine feet as part of the project to build the locks, a beach appeared. In response to Madrona residents' requests for a public swimming beach and recreational facilities, the City acquired the park in 1908. The bathhouse was built in 1926 for bathers. In 1971 it was converted into a dance studio, which has been enormously popular. Originally Lake Washington Boulevard divided the narrow park, but as automobile traffic increased the road was moved closer to the bluff to prevent accidents. Neighbors have contributed to the park's amenities, bringing in driftwood logs and sand for the beach and building a small hand pump to provide water for their tots' many construction projects in

the sand. In the summer refreshment stands sell barbequed ribs and snacks, enticing visitors to linger in the park. Local lore says that one dock is for geese and the other for people – but the geese don't seem to read the rules.

The Walk

It doesn't take long to walk this small 30-acre park, but stop and enjoy the exquisite views and envision the lake at its original level, lapping at the base of the hillside across the road. All these lakeshore walks would be nice for a canine companion on leash.

This walk is just a half-mile north of Leschi, page 169, so it could easily be combined with that walk. Or, for the more ambitious, it's two miles south of Madison Park, page 159, along sidewalks through the residential area.

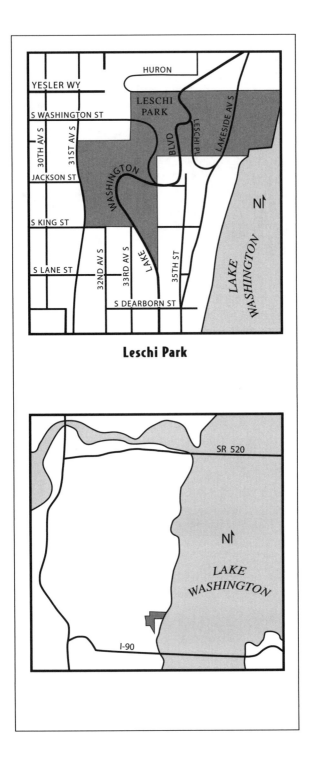

Leschi Park

LESCHI PARK

Distance	1 mile round trip
Time	½ - 1 hour
Terrain	Variable – broad paved paths and wooded trails
Restrooms	Seasonal
Food	Restaurants nearby

*T*he elegance of this park belies its colorful history as a spot for summer outings, a zoo and a dance hall. Now stately hedges and groomed ivy beds set off spectacular vistas across Lake Washington to Bellevue and the Cascades beyond.

Getting There

By Car: Drive east on Yesler Way to Thirty-second Avenue. Turn right at the Leschi bird totem onto Thirty-second and wind through Frink Park down to the shore of Lake Washington. Turn left onto Lakeside Avenue South and go about ¼ mile north to the marina on your right.

Or drive south on Lake Washington Boulevard to the park between Yesler and Main, near the Yacht Basin buildings.

Park along Lakeside Avenue South or in the parking lot. Note the signs about restricted parking for the marina.

Metro: Bus # 27.

Background

Geologists believe that an ancient landslide above Lake Washington created Leschi's steep hills and deep drop-off along the shore, which is unlike most of the lake's gradual shoreline.

Before Seattle's pioneers arrived the Nisqually tribe camped in the area. Their chief, Leschi, was one of the most outspoken Indian leaders against the white settlers. Accused of being an instigator of the Indian uprising over the 1855 Point Elliott Treaties, Leschi was arrested after the Indians' defeat and eventually hanged. Many felt he had been a scapegoat, and years later his name was cleared. This lovely park and neighborhood received his name.

Like other Seattle parks, Leschi Park was an amenity for a new tract developers built after they logged the land. Area residents commuted from businesses in downtown Seattle on a cable car operated by the Seattle Electric Company from the foot of Yesler Way, which went over Profanity Hill (present-day First Hill), across two miles of residential districts, and ended in a steep descent down to the park on the lake shore. After the turn of the century the park had a zoo, a dock for side-wheel steamers and boat rentals, a casino, magnificent gardens, and a dance pavilion where band concerts were held and plays were produced. The most famous actress of the time, Sarah Bernhardt, presented *Camille* in the pavilion theater in 1906. With no trees to block their view, people could see a panorama of the Cascades extending from Mount Rainier to Mount Baker from verandas and promenades. Summer beach cottages lined the beach in both directions from the park. Ferries transported passengers, and later cars, to Mercer Island and Medina, encouraging development on the Eastside.

In 1903 the Seattle Electric Company donated Leschi's zoo animals to the Woodland Park Zoo and a few years later sold the park itself to the city. The Olmsted Brothers firm designed the present more passive park as part of their extensive parks program along Lake Washington's shores in the early 1900s. The steamboats ceased their runs after the lake was lowered in 1916 and the construction of the original Floating Bridge in 1940 spelled the end of the cross-lake ferries.

The Walk

Note: Leschi Park is less than a mile from Madrona Park. You may wish to combine to two walks.

From the grassy area by the parking lot on Lakeside Avenue South look out on sailboats nestled in their docks. Cross the street and take one of the paved paths that curve gently uphill. After passing rose beds, clipped hedges, sweeping lawns and stately deciduous and evergreen trees, the paths converge in front of the brick restrooms. The centerpiece sequoia is set off with a plaque dedicating it to Jacob Umlaff who did so much for Seattle's parks.

Take the trail on the left and walk up to a play area and an expansive view to the east. Continue to the right (north) along Lake Washington Boulevard South. The park's tennis courts will be on your right below you, and straight ahead, a curious large concrete structure, the remains of the old cable car trestle.

Walk along the road and under the stout bridge. From the north side of the bridge look

uphill and see the route of the old Yesler Way cable car along the hillside. Most of the trestle was wood and decayed years ago; the concrete wall behind the tennis courts was the final leg of the trip to the lake shore. Listen for the echoes of the trolley car clanging its way down to the barn.

You may end your walk here if you wish: Walk downhill past the tennis courts to return to your car, parked near the site of the old casino.

Or, you may extend your walk through the woods across the street.

From the north side of the bridge, cross the road and find the trail up through the woods. The trail splits on the south side, giving you several choices. If you go to the right, up the steepest trail, you'll come out at Thirty-second Avenue, by the Leschi totem. The trails to the left are more gentle and have strategically placed benches to rest on. Depending on your route, you may pass a small waterfall.

Retrace your steps through the tall maples or walk down Lake Washington Boulevard to the tennis courts.

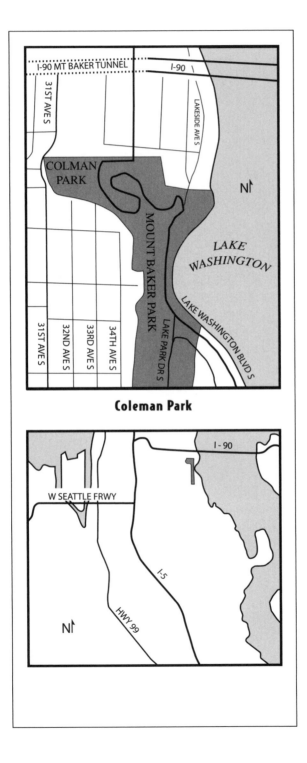

Coleman Park

COLMAN PARK

Distance	1 mile round trip
Time	1 hour
Terrain	Varying terrain – some paved paths. All uphill – or down hill
Restrooms	In adjacent Mount Baker Park
Food	No

*C*olman *Park shares much of its history with the adjacent Mount Baker Park – their boundaries, buildings and even names often intertwined. Starting with a pleasant waterfront sweep along Lake Washington, the park winds uphill along a steep ravine, under bridges and past tall trees and overgrown shrubs.*

Getting There

By Car: Head east on Yesler Way to Thirty-second Avenue. Turn right onto Thirty-second and wind through Frink Park down to the shore of Lake Washington. At Lakeside Drive South, turn right and head south for approximately one mile. Pass under I-90 and continue south. There is a sharp left turn into the Colman Park parking lot; or drive to the

Mount Baker lot, turn around, and drive back into the Colman lot a little to the north.

Or, drive along Lake Washington Boulevard heading south and stay by the lakeshore as it becomes Lakeside Avenue South.

Metro: Bus #27 runs at the bottom of Colman Park and #14 runs at the top.

Background

The early years of the 1900s were a time of enormous growth in Seattle. With logging completed on most of the west side of Lake Washington, developers began to turn their cleared properties into residential areas. To entice people to their new tracts some created parks along the Lake Washington shore; others donated pieces of property as civic gestures.

Most of this park was a gift from the James Colman estate in 1910. An energetic Scottish engineer, Colman came to Seattle in 1869 after working in sawmills on the west side of Puget Sound and leased the town's sawmill from Henry Yesler, then rebuilt it after it burned down in the Great Seattle Fire of 1889. He organized the Cedar Mountain Coal Company in 1884, which operated in eastern King County until 1940, and the Seattle & Walla Walla Railroad, which carried that coal out fifteen miles from Newcastle to Puget Sound, an enormously profitable undertaking. Colman was literally the "coal man," which made him a wealthy man in early Seattle.

In the late 1800s the Mount Baker Pumping Station supplied most of the city's water from its location on the north side of the present-day Colman Park. It once was the pump house of the Spring Hill Water Company, Seattle's first water company, which pumped lake water into wooden pipes serving city homes. The original building, built with rough boards painted dark red, was reached by a road that wound through the forest and hills. In 1886 James Colman repaired the pump after East Coast experts had failed. This is the same pump pressed into service for the Great Seattle Fire in 1889, but it was too small for the crisis. The following year the Cedar River Water System was developed for the city and the "Lake Washington Pumping Plant," as it came to be called, was placed on stand-by emergency basis. A new building, built in 1892 after the fire, was used after 1925 for storage and later as a community bathhouse. When the lake level dropped nine feet with the digging of the Montlake Cut, the old lake shore bulkhead was revealed.

In the early 1900s, about the same time that the Hunter Company donated Mount Baker Park as an amenity to their tract to the south, C.P. Dose donated some property for a small park. He built steps, which became known as Dose Terrace, from his adjoining tract to the north down to the lakefront, roughly in the middle of Mount Baker Park, which also included the pumping station and beach. As the park's popularity increased, additional facilities were added, with the unused pump station being remodeled into a bathhouse, rest rooms and storage facility for the Parks Department.

In 1965 the nearby boathouse in Mount Baker Park was remodeled into a bathhouse, and a swimming-fishing pier was added, finally putting Mount Baker Beach in Mount Baker Park. The old pump house building to the north was demolished and the park renamed in honor of James Colman, who had donated a strip of land along the side of his development. The Parks Department acquired the entire slope between Colman and Mount Baker

Parks, including Dose Terrace, in the 1980s after recurring landslides came through the area.

Designed by the Olmsteds, 27-acre Colman Park originally offered sweeping views of the lake and mountains beyond, which have been obscured by trees and ornamental shrubs as the years have passed. The Seattle Park Department, in conjunction with neighborhood groups, is doing extensive renovation on the park, clearing overgrown areas and restoring native plantings.

The Walk

Note: It is approximately 1¼ miles from Leschi Park to Colman Park, along a scenic residential sidewalk. The cross streets dead-end at the lake shore, with small parks and benches overlooking the lake. The new Day Street park has recently been created under the I-90 freeway.

Begin the hike from the parking lot by the shore sheltered with weeping willows. You can get your bearings from a map of the park at the south end of the parking lot. Duck under the bridge at Lakeside Avenue South and through another moss-covered underpass at Lake Washington Boulevard South. Continue straight up through the grass and shrubs on a steep footpath to the left. Look for a wide trail that swings in a horseshoe through woods, then turns uphill until it intersects the upper switchback of the road below the small Park Department nursery.

Stay on the path, under the bridge, a Victorian nineteenth century design with flaring steps. When the park was new this had a wide view of Lake Washington, now obscured by mature maple trees. Look for the frog pond on the left. Like much of this park, the Parks Department is restoring the habitat and hopes

the pond will soon be filled with croaking frogs again. Just beyond, in the clearing, a terraced neighborhood P-Patch garden yields sunflowers, corn, pumpkins, dahlias, grapes, and nasturtiums, as well as a small garden for a local food bank. The wetland was converted to a series of ponds.

Continue hiking to the top of the gardens. On both sides there are almost-hidden very steep stairs. Whew! Keep climbing on either set of stairs and come out on Thirty-first Avenue South; the north stairway at Massachusetts Street and the south at South Holgate Street (#14 bus stop). From the road you can barely see over the tops of the tall trees to the wonderful view of Lake Washington and the Cascades that once was visible from lower in the park.

Return to the lakeshore by a different route, and, as you emerge from the woods, enjoy the expansive view of Lake Washington. Walk to the north side of the parking lot, where you'll see a balustrade, a recent addition, above the remains of the old pump house. If you walk south, along the lakeshore path toward Mount Baker Park (about a quarter of a mile), you'll see the steps to Dose Terrace across the street.

James W. Colman

James Colman came to the U.S. in 1854 from his native Scotland where he was an engineer. He settled in Wisconsin, found work as engineer and married a girl also from Scotland. In 1861 he came to the Puget Sound country to "establish a place for himself," leaving his wife and two sons behind. An exceedingly hard worker, he first managed the Port Madison sawmill for three years, then purchased the Port Orchard mill, which burned down in 1868. He moved to Seattle and purchased Yesler's mill, which was not operating at the time, and became a wealthy man and a civic leader. Historian F. Grant wrote that: "for ten years the history of Mr. Colman is the history of Seattle."

After establishing himself and his business enterprises, he brought his family to Seattle in 1882 and took his sons into his businesses: He took the lead in building Seattle's first railroad to the coal mines near Renton, then extended it to Newcastle, providing both the engineering and the capital for the road. He owned many buildings, some destroyed and rebuilt after the Fire, including the Colman Building at Columbia and First Avenue and the Colman Dock. His sons inherited his enterprises after his death in 1906.

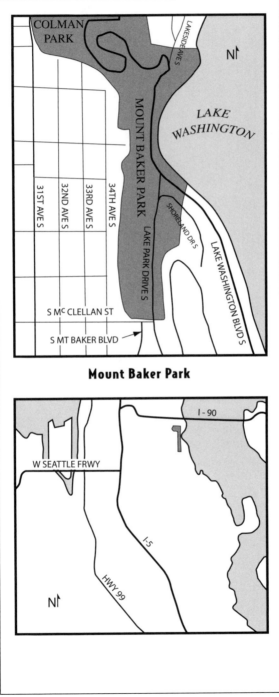

Mount Baker Park

MOUNT BAKER PARK

Distance	¾+ mile round trip
Time	1 hour
Terrain	A gentle hill
Restrooms	At the beach and in the upper park
Food	Restaurants nearby

*S*tarting in a cove on the south end of Lake Washington, Mount Baker Park wanders across the street, heads uphill along a shaded stream, and, at it highest point, ends up by tennis courts and a children's play area. In the summer the beach is the main attraction, but year-round this gracious park and neighborhood are lovely to visit.*

Getting There

By Car: From I-5, take I-90. Get off at the first exit, Rainier Avenue South. Go approximately half a mile. Turn left at McClellan (a major intersection). Just after the stoplight at Mount Rainier Drive, turn left onto Mount Baker Boulevard There is a large parking lot by the lakeshore and two small parking lots along the road, or you can park on neighboring side streets.

You can also reach this area by driving along Lake Washington Boulevard, heading south along the Lake Washington shore to South McClellan.

Or, from the west, follow tree-lined Mount Baker Boulevard from Rainier Drive South past Franklin High School (on the Seattle Historic Preservation Register) to Lake Park Drive. Park in the small Mount Baker parking lot.

Metro: Bus # 14 goes to the top of the park.

Background

Pioneer David Denny originally owned this eleven-and-a-half-acre ravine and lake-front beach. He sold the property to developer James Colman, who later sold it to the Hunter Tract Improvement Company. They envisioned an exclusive private beach and residential area and hired the prominent Olmsted Brothers firm to design their Mount Baker Subdivision, which included both the park and the Hunter Tract above it. The development was laid out to take advantage of lake and mountain views by following the hillside topography. Houses and lots had to meet minimum sizes and farm animals were prohibited. In 1908, shortly before Lake Washington Boulevard was completed, the lower part of the tract was donated to the city for a park. By the 1920s the beach had become another public attraction, but unlike Leschi or Madison parks, it was never meant to be a resort. For a few years in the 1950s, Mount Baker's docks were race headquarters for the Seafair Unlimited Hydroplane races, which have since been moved a couple of miles to Stan Sayres Park. When the bathhouse in the nearby Colman Park deteriorated it was replaced with the red brick Mount Baker Beach Bathhouse.

Today Mount Baker Park has year-round use by those who walk through its gentle ravine and who enjoy feeling the shoreline belongs to them. Swimmers fill the small beach in the summer months, and boats and fishermen use the wooden dock. Bicycle Sunday riding days begin from the north part of the park.

The Walk

Note: This walk can easily be combined with the Colman Park walk, page175.

Start at the beach. To the east you can see the Cascades and Bellevue's skyscrapers, and to the north, the floating bridge. Then turn and notice the old concrete bulkhead along the shoreline supporting the road and curved beach. A recent concrete balustrade, similar to the one in Colman Park, with built-in formal lights reflecting its Olmsted heritage, leads back up to the road. Look for the small plaque at the base of north light from the Friends of Olmsted Parks. Their contributions helped pay for the new lights in the 1980s.

Cross the street to the winding paved path and follow the stream and ponds uphill past landscaped flower beds to the old stone pagoda, suitably framed by Japanese maples and Portuguese laurel. When Seattle sent its first delegation to visit Japan at the turn of the century, one of the members admired the Japanese stone lanterns and asked to take one home. He was discouraged by his hosts, but afterward they sent this stone lantern as a gift to the city. Later Kojiro Matsukata, a Japanese dignitary, came to see it in this beautiful setting in Mount Baker Park.

Walk uphill, past the stream and series of small landscaped ponds. Cooperating community groups have restored a series of above-ground working weirs and pools, much like

those in England. Native trees, such as cedars, maples, firs and alders, stand beside introduced trees such as cherries, redwoods, horse chestnuts and weeping hemlocks.

Continue walking along the stream to reach the play area and tennis courts.

The top of the park is at South McClellan Street, named for George McClellan who is remembered locally for having surveyed the way across Snoqualmie Pass in 1852. Later he became better known as one of Lincoln's Civil War generals.

Beyond the children's play area at the top of the park there is a short trail to the residential area, with some of the city's most gracious homes. Walk east along McClellan for half a block to the intersection with Mount Rainier Place and Mount Baker Boulevard South. A small paved trail winds uphill, so hidden by ivy and big trees it is easy to miss. Walk in any direction along Mount St. Helens Place and adjoining streets and imagine turn-of-the-century bicyclists wheeling around the curves.

The community center around the corner and small deli on McClellan Street and Mount Baker Boulevard are gathering spots for neighbors and visitors. If you would like to extend your walk, you may walk along Mount Baker Boulevard as it curves through the neighborhood before returning to your car.

When you return to the beach, walk out on the dock and survey Seattle's amazing parks: Colman, Mount Baker and Seward. Thank visionary turn-of-the-century civic leaders and the Olmsted Brothers firm for our beautiful city.

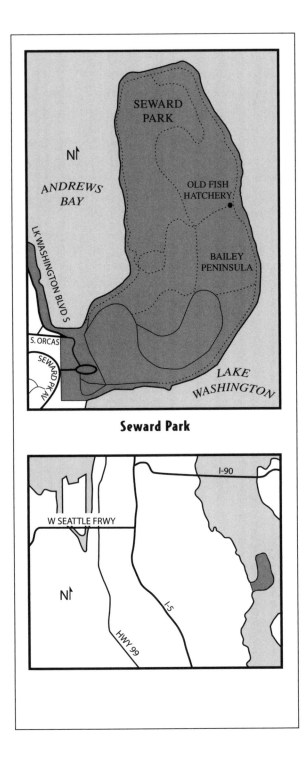

Seward Park

SEWARD PARK

Distance	2 - 4 miles round trip
Time	2+ hours
Terrain	Beach – level; woods – hilly
Restrooms	By parking and picnic areas
Food	Snack cart in summer

*T*ucked away at the south end of Lake Washington is one of Seattle's most diverse parks. With its broad sheltered beach, sunny shoreline, forest paths, and expansive views, this large wilderness park on the edge of the city has something for everyone.

Getting There

By Car: From I-5 take Exit 163 to South Columbian Way. Take a right on Beacon Avenue South, then take a left on South Orcas Street. At the bottom of the hill, take a right into the park.

A more scenic approach is to drive south along Lake Washington Boulevard, passing other lakeshore parks, from either Madison or Yesler streets until it ends at Seward Park.

Metro: Bus #39.

Background

Before the level of Lake Washington was low-ered nine feet, the Bailey Peninsula was barely accessible, connected to Seattle by a narrow spine of land. But even then, E. O. Schwagerl, Seattle's first park supervisor, recognized it as a perfect location for a park, "suitable for the pub-lic pleasure," as it has been ever since. In fact, at the turn of the century Schwagerl proposed sell-ing Volunteer Park, which was high and dry, so the city could afford to buy this peninsula.

A few years later, when the Olmsted Brothers firm laid out Seattle's park system in the early 1900s, they too selected the Bailey Peninsula for a park site as part of their Comprehensive System of Parks and Parkways for Seattle. The city finally bought the land after the Alaska-Yukon-Pacific Exposition in 1909 and named the park after William Seward, the Secretary of State who had pur-chased Alaska for the U.S. (His statue had been prominently displayed at the A-Y-P and was moved to Volunteer Park after the fair, where it still stands, in spite of periodic efforts to move it to Seward Park.)

Only a tiny neck of land originally con-nected the peninsula to the mainland, but in 1916, when the Montlake Cut lowered Lake Washington, the neck between the park and the mainland broadened, improving access. Following the Olmsted Plan for Seward Park, trails were cut through the woods connecting with picnic groves, a dance pavilion, play-ground, a bathing beach and bathhouses, and piers for boats and fishing. The access road was filled and expanded, and the three miles of shoreland approaching the park was widened, creating the gracious approach along Lake Washington. Public facilities developed around the south end of the park. A road along the shore encircles the park, but was closed to cars in the 1950s.

Most of the park's development came in the 1920s and 1930s, when a concession stand, tennis courts, restrooms with changing rooms for bathers, and beach improvements were built. Gifts of flowering cherry trees and the large stone lantern enhanced the park and boulevard. During the Depression years funds from government projects enlarged the bathhouse, built the retaining wall around the shore, and created fish-rearing ponds to make Lake Washington a "fisherman's paradise." (Now closed, the pump house and ponds are on the east side of the park.) Some clearing and logging was done at the time. The area's biggest trees had been logged earlier, leaving smaller trees behind, now some of the oldest in the city.

Before World War II Indians often came to the park for canoe races and other tribal events.

The park's popular outdoor stage led to the creation of the amphitheatre in the 1950s to accommodate summer concerts. Alas, they were too popular, creating huge traffic problems for the nearby neighborhoods, and were discontinued. Nowadays the amphitheatre remains popular for smaller events, such as the Rainier District PowWow Days where tribe members participate in canoe races and other tribal events. The bathhouse has become an arts center, like the one in Madrona Park. The park remains a remote beach and woodland escape on the edge of the city.

An eight-ton stone Japanese lantern, called the Taiko Gata, was presented by the citizens of Yokohama in gratitude for the help Seattleites gave the Japanese people after their earthquake of 1923. It was placed next to the Japanese cherries at the north entrance. Later they gave Seattle 3,500 more cherry trees, which were divided among all Seattle parks; some can still be found here. Look also for a stone torii, or gateway, bearing the legend "Seattle's Gateway to the Orient" placed near the stone lantern in 1934.

Bikers and skaters share the broad paved path along the shore with strollers and joggers. The sheltered gravel beach is popular during the summer. Trails crisscross the park's forested interior, a reminder of how the area looked 100 years ago. Some are steep and lead to high vantage points, up to picnic grounds, and to the old fish hatchery, now closed.

Bikes are prohibited on forest trails, but allowed on paved roads; note the one-way signs.

During the summer boat races and water-ski exhibits attract crowds to the waterfront, as do baseball games and band concerts on the fields and in the amphitheatre. A women's triathalon has been held in Seward Park in recent years. A canine companion on leash would be welcome on the waterfront roadway.

The Walk

There are three very different walks in this 322-acre park: one is hilly and cool, on trails through the trees; another is a broad, paved promenade along the shore. A paved road for cars circles the ridge of the park and leads to the amphitheatre and picnic tables, with some walkways. Kiosks along the way have trail maps.

For the forest walk: Begin walking on the path leading uphill from the torii or along the road beside it. Either will lead you to a sheltered picnic area looking down over Andrews Bay, named for W. R. Andrews, who was an early homesteader and Park Board commissioner. At the top of the hill, just beyond this fork, is the amphitheater, an idyllic spot for summer concerts.

Dirt, or muddy, trails lead from the picnic area into the woods. The farther you walk into the forest the harder it is to believe you are still in Seattle, not in the mountains. A tangle of native trees and shrubs, Douglas firs, western red cedars, Pacific madronas, and western hemlocks obscure the light on all but the brightest days. Woodpeckers, jays and flickers search the old stumps for insect life.

You may also follow the paved road for cars, which makes a loop around the crown of the park starting by the upper picnic area. This three-quarter mile walk climbs slightly as it passes by the amphitheater and has occasional peeks of vistas to the south and east through the mature trees.

An alternative is the level two-and-a-half mile shore road. First opened in 1921, the road was expanded in 1948 as a one-way loop for bicyclists. Today it is used year round by runners, skaters, bicyclists, and children. During one 10K race a few years ago members of the Seattle Symphony played their instruments one at a time at different stations along this loop. At the finish line trumpets played a fanfare based on the "Hallelujah Chorus." William Seward would have been amazed.

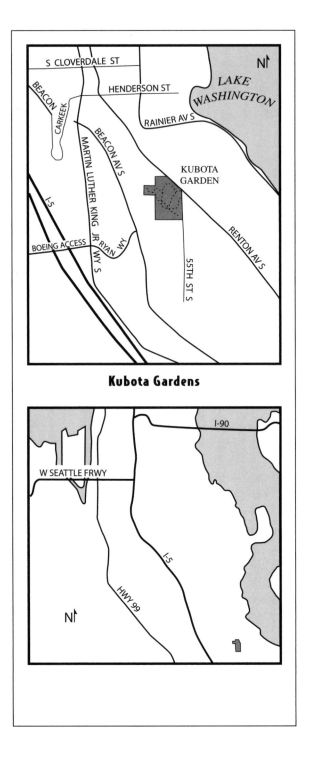

Kubota Gardens

KUBOTA GARDENS

Distance	1 - 2 miles round trip
Time	1 hour
Terrain	Varied: A broad level pathway and narrow winding trails
Restrooms	Sanican
Food	No

O ne of the largest Japanese gardens in the country, this jewel of a city park reflects our Asian community's history and the garden's past as a nursery. Tucked away in the Beacon Hill neighborhood, the garden is a tribute to its founder's hard work, vision and skill.

Getting There

By Car: From downtown Seattle, take I-5 south and exit at Exit 161A, Albro Place. Turn left at the traffic light and cross the freeway. Turn right onto Swift Avenue South. Drive one mile and turn right on Beacon Avenue South. Drive one mile and turn left on Cloverdale. Drive one-half mile and turn right on Renton Avenue South. Continue for a mile, then turn right onto Fifty-fifth Street

South (there is a Seattle Parks sign), which leads directly to Kubota Gardens on the right.

Metro: Bus #106 goes to Renton Avenue South and Fifty-fourth Street.

Background

Located in the south end of Seattle, this beautiful park was once a commercial nursery run by the Kubota family. Fujitaro Kubota, a farmer from Japan, had studied agriculture and the old temples and gardens of Kochi Prefec-ture. He emigrated to Seattle in 1907 and began a landscape business, purchasing the initial five acres for the nursery in 1927. With his family, Mr. Kubota developed an outstanding landscaped garden as a demonstration exhibit for customers, using Northwest native plant materials and traditional Japanese design. He was a pioneer in Japanese landscaping in Seattle.

The Kubotas were one of many Japanese-American families sent to internment camps during World War II, and the garden was left untended for the years of their absence. When Mr. Kubota returned he resurrected the garden and expanded the ponds, streams, waterfall, and rock garden. Many plants needed drastic pruning and some had died in the interim. It is said that when visitors would ask Mr. Kubota for the name of the species of some plant, he would reply in Japanese "I don't know," and they would think he had given the correct species name.

Because of his skill, he was invited to help landscape the Seattle University campus and the Bloedel Reserve. For over fifty years the Kubota Gardens remained in business with family members caring for the unusual collection of trees, shrubs, and flowers. People came from long distances to buy specimen plants and trees from the Kubota family.

In 1987 the City of Seattle purchased the grounds, which had grown to twenty acres, for a city park, and the Kubota Garden Foundation was established in 1989 to support the maintenance of the garden.

Since it has become a park, it has given many people joy and pleasure to walk among the weeping trees and enjoy the waterfalls and ponds. Because of the garden's age, mature trees that were contorted years ago have grown gnarled and twisted in very unusual ways. Some are almost horizontal and lie close to the ground. Look for many kinds of Japanese maples, weeping gray-needled Atlas cedars, Deodar cedars that seem almost to be ground covers, red and black pines, yellow, black and variegated bamboo, and cypresses. In the fall the burning bush turns bright crimson. In the spring the cherry trees fill the sky with cloud-like blossoms. Massive rocks found locally are placed throughout the garden to enhance the landscape.

The Walk

There is a trail map showing the park's layout and information by the parking lot. A canine companion on leash would be welcome on the broader paths.

Although it is one of the largest Japanese-style gardens in the country, it has a surprisingly intimate feeling. The walks through the gardens vary from narrow, twisting paths to wide walkways and bridges. The narrow trails meander through stunningly beautiful plantings with each new bend in the trail opening to another jewel-like vista – some with benches tucked in almost-hidden crannies. Streams and waterfalls weave around and under the trails, bridged with natural rock stepping stones and formal red lacquered bridges. Be sure to cross the red

arched Moon Bridge and climb the "Moun-
tainside" to see the vista over the garden and
the Necklace of Ponds far below. Many
white-veiled brides have been photographed
here or in front of one of remarkable trees.

A new addition to the garden honors Tom
Kubota, son of Fujitaro, who worked in the
business and in the garden with his father. This
broad, flat pathway is especially dedicated to
senior citizens who might have difficulty with
some of the steeper trails.

QUICK REFERENCE

The following table gives a general idea of the walks and terrain. Some walks may have food in summer, but not be marked because we want readers to be able to plan for their trips and not be caught short. Several walks have split personalities, with broad level pathways in one part and steeper trails in another. Regarding dogs and wheelchair accessibility, people may feel comfortable with pets and strollers in places that are not marked. Use this chart as a general guide – quick look at what various walks offer.

Walk	Page	Distance (miles)	Time (hours)	Difficulty	Food	Nature	Wheelchairs & Stollers	Art	Dogs (on leash)
Alki	15	6+	2–3	easy	🍃	🍃	🍃	🍃	🍃
Lincoln Park	25	1¾	2	easy/hilly		🍃	🍃		🍃
Schmitz Park	31	1–2	1	hilly	🍃	🍃		🍃	🍃
Waterfront	37	1¼	1	easy			🍃	🍃	
Myrtle Edwards Park	49	3	1	easy	🍃	🍃	🍃	🍃	🍃
Pike Place Market	55	1	2+	moderate	🍃				
Downtown	67	1	1	easy	🍃				
Pioneer Square	75	1	1+	easy	🍃		🍃	🍃	
International District	89	1½	1½–2	mod/hill	🍃			🍃	
West Capitol Hill	105	3	1–2	variable		🍃			
Volunteer Park	115	2	1–2	moderate		🍃	🍃	🍃	🍃

	Page			Terrain					
Lake View Cemetery	123	2	1½–2	moderate					🍃
East Capitol Hill	129	2½–3	2–2½	moderate	🍃				
Interlaken	137	3	1–2	moderate		🍃	🍃		🍃
First Hill	143	1½	2–2½	moderate	🍃			🍃	
Central District	153	2	2	mod-hilly	🍃				
Madison Park	165	½	½	easy	🍃	🍃	🍃		🍃
Madrona Park	171	½	½	easy		🍃	🍃		🍃
Leschi Park	175	1	½–1	mod-hilly	🍃	🍃	🍃		🍃
Colman Park	181	1	1	mod-hilly		🍃	🍃		🍃
Mount Baker Park	189	¾+	1	mod-hilly	🍃	🍃			🍃
Seward Park	195								
–beach		2	2	level	🍃	🍃	🍃		🍃
–trails		1–2	1+	hilly	🍃	🍃			
Kabota Park	201	1–2	1	level-mod		🍃	🍃		🍃

INDEX